KitchenAid®
CONVECTION COLLECTION

112 Recipes and Tips for Making the Most of Your New Oven

This seal assures you that every recipe in *KitchenAid® Convection Collection* has been tested in the *Better Homes and Gardens®* Test Kitchen. This means that each recipe is practical and reliable, and meets high standards of taste appeal.

Pictured on the cover: Herb-Crusted Roast Pork (recipe, page 36), Gruyère-Pecan Biscuits (recipe, page 72), Savory Rosemary Scones (recipe, page 73), and Lemon Curd Pastry with Mixed Berries (recipe, page 76).

Juicy...Golden...Flaky...Tender...Airy... Moist...Consistently Excellent...

Do these words describe the foods you love? Then you'll enjoy your new *KitchenAid® Thermal-Convection™* oven and this collection of delicious recipes and valuable advice.

With the straightforward guide on pages 3 to 5 and the handy baking tips and cooking charts throughout the book, you'll achieve convection perfection from the start. You'll also prize this selection of recipes; many are sure to become part of your everyday cooking repertoire.

From potpies for everyday enjoyment to elegant dishes for guests, you'll appreciate the difference your *KitchenAid®* convection oven brings to all the meals you create—a difference you'll love.

Table of Contents

The Basics of Convection Cooking

Convection ovens were first used by chefs in restaurants because the ovens allowed them to cook large quantities of food evenly and efficiently. Now, you have this same technology in your own home.

A convection oven differs from a standard thermal oven because it has a fan that keeps hot air continuously moving throughout the oven cavity. This movement of hot air cooks foods more evenly and efficiently. Cooking times, especially for large roasts and poultry, are shortened by as much as 30 percent.

Convection Cooking Advantages

Although cooking foods quickly is important, *KitchenAid*® convection ovens also have these significant advantages.

- They consistently achieve superior results with baked, roasted, and broiled foods.

  Meats and poultry roast to an even, golden brown, and poultry develops a deliciously crisp skin. The circulating hot air seals the surface of the meat or poultry so more juices are retained.

  Baked chicken pieces and fish turn out moist and tender on the inside and evenly done on the outside. If the pieces are coated, they bake to crispy perfection.

  Yeast breads are crustier and more uniformly golden brown than those baked in standard ovens.

  There's no need to shield the crusts on pies and tarts with foil because they bake evenly.

  Convection broiling seals in the natural flavor and moisture of foods.

- Convection ovens save energy because even heating allows you to cook most foods at lower oven temperatures.

- Convection ovens are convenient—you can bake or roast a number of foods on several racks all at the same time.

- Convection ovens heat evenly at very low temperatures, so you can dry fruits, vegetables, and herbs to enjoy all year.

Cook Settings

Your *KitchenAid*® convection oven has three convection cook settings—Convection Roast, Convection Bake, and Convection Broil. Here's how to use each to the best advantage.

Convection Bake

On the Convection Bake setting the ring element behind the back wall operates when heating and the fan circulates the air for even cooking. This setting is ideal for baking breads, cakes, and delicate items such as soufflés. It's also well suited for baking several items at once using two or three rack positions.

When using the Convection Bake setting, first position the racks so the top of the food is in the center of the oven. Rack positions 2 and 3 usually work best, but for tall items, such as angel food cakes, you may need to use position 1. Then preheat the oven until it signals that it has reached the correct temperature.

Convection Roast

On the Convection Roast setting the bake element underneath the floor of the oven and the outer top element operate when heating. The fan circulates air evenly in the oven. This setting is used for roasting meats and poultry and for baking some desserts.

To roast meats or poultry, position an oven rack so the top of the food will be in the center of the oven. For most foods, use rack position 2. For very large roasts or turkeys, you may need to use position 1.

Place the convection roasting rack on top of the two-piece broiler pan, then place the food on the rack. This holds the food above the sides of the pan so air circulates around the food for better browning. There's no need to preheat the oven for roasting meats and poultry, simply place the pan of food in the oven, close the door, and set the correct oven temperature.

When Convection Roast is used to bake pies and other pastries that need tender, flaky crusts, follow the preheating directions in the recipe.

Convection Broil

On the Convection Broil setting the top elements operate at full power when heating and the fan circulates air. The combination of circulating hot air and the direct heat of the broil elements browns and cooks broiled foods evenly, including thick cuts of meat.

The Convection Broil temperature is preset at 450°F but can be set at variable temperatures. To broil, preheat the oven at the desired temperature about 5 minutes. Place the food on the unheated, two-piece broiler pan and set it in the oven. Always close the door for convection broiling.

Rack position 4 is normally used for broiling. However, you can vary the rack position as well as the temperature to achieve the results you prefer. For thicker cuts of meat and poultry, you may want to use a rack position farther from the broiling elements. Convection Broil times will vary depending on rack position and temperature.

Convection Dehydration

Your convection oven can be used for drying top-quality fruits, vegetables, and herbs. A book specifically on dehydration would be a good source for detailed information.

The size of the food pieces, moisture content of the food, amount of food being dried at one time, and humidity in the air all affect the length of time it will take to dehydrate. Always check foods for doneness early in the cycle. Cool items to room temperature before testing for doneness.

Food should be placed on a closely woven open-grid rack so air can circulate around all the surfaces of the food and dry evenly. The close weave on the grid also prevents foods from falling through. It is important that the rack is able to withstand the heat and moisture from the food.

Convection Cookware

There's no need to buy special dishes and baking pans for your convection oven. For most foods, standard bakeware works fine. Here are a few cookware pointers for convection cooking:

- When choosing baking pans, keep in mind that shiny pans give baked goods a light, tender crust, while dull, dark metal pans or glass baking dishes give a deeper color and a more crusty surface.

- Be sure to use cookie sheets without sides in your convection oven. These sheets let air circulate around the cookies so they brown more evenly.

- If you use insulated baking pans and cookie sheets, you may need to increase baking times. Baked goods do not brown as quickly in insulated pans as they do in regular utensils. Cookies baked on insulated cookie sheets may spread more. Bar cookies in insulated baking pans may not cook as quickly in the center. Insulated pans work well for rich breads that tend to get very brown on the bottom.

Remember these useful tips when using your *KitchenAid*® convection oven.

- Position the racks in your oven before you turn it on. Then you won't be handling hot oven racks.

- Preheat the oven if the recipe specifies a preheated oven. Otherwise, it is not necessary to preheat.

- Position foods as close to the center of the oven as possible, being sure to leave space between the pans and the oven walls so hot air can circulate around the food.

- You can convection cook on several racks at the same time for example, three cookie sheets or four round cake pans. In 30- and 27-inch ovens, six pies can be convection cooked at the same time on three racks.

- Dishes are left uncovered for convection cooking to allow the circulating air to brown and crisp the foods. If you wish to prepare one of your own recipes that calls for the dish to be covered, you can either convection cook or standard bake the food. The baking temperature and time for a covered dish baked by convection will probably be about the same as for standard baking. If the dish bakes for an extended time, you may reduce the temperature by 25°F to 50°F for convection cooking.

- To avoid loss of heat and temperature fluctuation, open the oven door as little as possible during baking.

- Always test for doneness a few minutes before the minimum time given in the recipe, especially for baked goods. Use the doneness test given in the recipe. The fact that the food looks golden brown is not a reliable test. Foods cooked in a 24-inch convection oven will probably be ready in the minimum time. Those baked in a 30-inch oven may take the maximum time.

Leek Appetizer Tart (see recipe, page 8)

Entertaining Specialties

Entertain family and friends in style with impressive dishes from your KitchenAid® convection oven. For dinner parties, select from outstanding entrées and desserts such as golden Cheese-Stuffed Chicken in Phyllo, succulent Pork Medaillons with Brandy-Cream Sauce, and perfectly browned Strudel Sticks. For casual parties, bake up savory tidbits like crispy Nacho Potato Skins and flaky Leek Appetizer Tart. Entertaining is sure to be a success with the terrific recipes in this collection.

Leek Appetizer Tart

Elegant, yet easy to prepare, the eye-catching slices of this luscious tart will make a zesty addition to any appetizer buffet. (Pictured on pages 6–7.)

1 egg
1 cup ricotta cheese (8 ounces)
3 tablespoons grated Parmesan or Romano cheese, divided
1 tablespoon milk
⅛ teaspoon pepper
3 medium leeks, sliced ½ inch thick (about 1 cup)
1 clove garlic, minced
1 tablespoon olive oil or cooking oil
¼ cup drained, chopped oil-pack dried tomatoes
1 sheet frozen puff pastry (½ of a 17¼-ounce package), thawed
1 teaspoon water
   Small fresh oregano leaves (optional)

Separate egg, reserving the egg white. For filling, in a small bowl combine egg yolk, ricotta cheese, *2 tablespoons* of the Parmesan cheese, the milk, and pepper. Stir until smooth.

In a medium saucepan cook leeks and garlic in oil about 5 minutes or until tender. Stir leek mixture and dried tomatoes into ricotta mixture. Set filling aside.

On a lightly floured surface, unfold pastry and roll into a 15x10-inch rectangle. Cut rectangle in half lengthwise. Cut off two ¾-inch-wide strips crosswise, then two ¾-inch-wide strips lengthwise from each rectangle. Set aside the 8 pastry strips.

Place the 2 pastry rectangles on a large baking sheet. In a small bowl combine egg white and water; brush onto rectangles. Place the 8 pastry strips on edges of rectangles to form a border and build up the sides, trimming to fit. Brush strips with egg white mixture. Prick bottoms of pastry with the tines of a fork.

Convection Roast in a preheated **375°F** oven for 10 minutes. (Or, standard bake in a preheated 375°F oven for 15 minutes.)

Spoon filling into baked pastry rectangles; spread to edges. Sprinkle with the remaining 1 tablespoon Parmesan cheese.

Convection Roast about 8 minutes more or until filling is set. (Or, standard bake for 10 to 15 minutes more.) Bias-slice rectangles crosswise. Serve warm. If desired, garnish with oregano leaves.
Makes 16 appetizer servings.

Cheese-Sauced Potato Skins

Crispy potato skins, perfectly roasted in the convection oven, are a terrific combo with the smooth cheese topping.

4	medium baking potatoes (about 1½ pounds total)
¼	cup butter or margarine, melted
¾	cup shredded cheddar or American cheese (3 ounces)
3	tablespoons all-purpose flour
½	teaspoon dry mustard
	Dash paprika
½	cup beer or milk
	Few dashes bottled hot pepper sauce
1	to 2 tablespoons milk
4	slices bacon, crisp-cooked, drained, and crumbled
2	green onions, sliced

Scrub potatoes, pat dry, and prick with fork.

Convection Bake in a **425°F** oven for 45 to 50 minutes or until tender. (Or, standard bake in a 425°F oven for 50 to 60 minutes.)

Cut potatoes lengthwise into quarters. Scoop out the insides (reserve for another use), leaving ⅜-inch-thick shells. Cut potato quarters crosswise in half. Brush both sides of potato pieces with melted butter. Place potato pieces, cut side up, on a 15x10x1-inch baking pan.

Convection Bake about 12 minutes more or until crisp. (Or, standard bake about 12 minutes more.)

Toss together cheese, flour, dry mustard, and paprika. In a saucepan heat beer and hot pepper sauce just until warm. Gradually add cheese mixture, stirring constantly over medium-low heat until cheese is melted. Stir in the 1 to 2 tablespoons milk to make a sauce of desired consistency. Serve over potato skins. Top with bacon and onions.
Makes 8 appetizer servings.

Nacho Potato Skins

Unexpected company? Surprise them with a heaping platter of these crisp Tex-Mex snacks. They're also great for a party or as a special treat for the family.

6	small baking potatoes (about 1½ pounds total)
¼	cup butter or margarine, melted
¾	cup shredded cheddar cheese (3 ounces)
2	green onions, sliced
	Prepared salsa or picante sauce

Scrub potatoes, pat dry, and prick with fork.

Convection Bake in a **425°F** oven for 35 to 40 minutes or until tender. (Or, standard bake in a 425°F oven for 40 to 50 minutes.)

Cut potatoes lengthwise into quarters. Scoop out the insides (reserve for another use), leaving ⅜-inch-thick shells. Brush both sides of potato quarters with melted butter.

Place potato quarters, cut side up, on a large baking sheet.

Convection Bake about 12 minutes or until crisp. (Or, standard bake about 12 minutes.) Sprinkle cheese and onions over the wedges.

Convection Bake for 1 to 2 minutes more or until cheese melts. (Or, standard bake for 1 to 2 minutes more.) Serve with salsa.
Makes 10 appetizer servings.

Polynesian Meatballs

Served with fruit chunks, these appealing tidbits are sure to satisfy hungry appetites.

  1   egg, beaten
  ¼   cup fine dry bread crumbs
  2   tablespoons snipped fresh cilantro or
         parsley
  2   cloves garlic, minced
  ¼   teaspoon salt
  ⅛   teaspoon ground red pepper
  1   pound lean ground beef
  ¼   cup finely chopped peanuts
  1   fresh pineapple or 2 papayas, peeled and
         cut into bite-size chunks, or one 20-ounce
         can pineapple chunks, drained
1¼   cups prepared sweet-and-sour sauce

In a large bowl combine egg, bread crumbs, cilantro, garlic, salt, and red pepper. Add ground beef and peanuts; mix well. Shape into 1-inch meatballs. For easier cleanup, line a 15x10x1-inch baking pan with foil. Place meatballs in foil-lined pan.

Convection Bake in a preheated **350°F** oven for 9 to 11 minutes or until meat is no longer pink. (Or, standard bake in a preheated 350°F oven about 20 minutes.) Drain off fat.

Thread a pineapple chunk and a meatball onto a wooden toothpick. Return to baking pan. Repeat with the remaining fruit and meatballs. Brush with some of the sweet-and-sour sauce.

Convection Bake for 3 to 4 minutes more or until heated through. (Or, standard bake for 5 to 8 minutes more.) In a small saucepan heat the remaining sauce until bubbly. Serve sauce with meatball skewers.
Makes about 42.

Fresh Basil and Tomato Pizza

The fresh ingredients in this vegetarian pizza give it a vibrant flavor.

  1   16-ounce loaf frozen bread dough, thawed
  1   cup shredded mozzarella cheese (4 ounces)
  ⅓   cup thinly sliced fresh basil leaves
  5   red and/or yellow plum tomatoes or
         3 medium tomatoes, sliced ¼ inch thick
  ¼   cup freshly grated Parmesan cheese
  ⅛   to ¼ teaspoon freshly ground pepper
         Small fresh basil leaves (optional)

On a lightly floured surface, roll bread dough into a 12-inch circle. Place in a 12-inch pizza pan, pressing dough to build up an edge. Using kitchen scissors, snip edge of crust every 1½ inches, angling cuts alternately left and right. Prick crust with the tines of a fork.

Convection Bake in a preheated **375°F** oven for 14 to 16 minutes or until golden brown. (Or, standard bake in a preheated 400°F oven for 14 to 16 minutes.)

Sprinkle crust with mozzarella cheese. Top with sliced basil, then tomato slices. Sprinkle with Parmesan cheese and pepper.

Convection Bake about 8 minutes more or until mozzarella cheese is melted and Parmesan cheese is lightly browned. (Or, standard bake about 8 minutes more.)

If desired, arrange basil leaves on pizza. Cut pizza into wedges.
Makes 12 appetizer servings.

Fresh Basil and Tomato Pizza

Crab and Havarti Quiche

Pastry for Single-Crust Pie (see recipe, page 81)
3 eggs, beaten
1½ cups milk
2 green onions, sliced
¼ teaspoon salt
⅛ teaspoon pepper
Dash ground nutmeg
¾ cup chopped cooked crabmeat or chicken
1½ cups shredded Havarti or Swiss cheese (6 ounces)
1 tablespoon all-purpose flour

Prepare Pastry for Single-Crust Pie. On a lightly floured surface, roll dough into a 12-inch circle. Fit into a 9-inch pie plate, being careful not to stretch pastry. Trim to ½ inch beyond edge of pie plate; fold under extra pastry. Make a high fluted edge.

Line pastry with a double thickness of foil, then add enough dry beans to cover plate bottom and hold down foil.

Convection Roast in a preheated **425°F** oven for 8 minutes. (Or, standard bake in a preheated 450°F oven for 8 minutes.) Remove beans and foil. (*Do not* reuse beans in cooking.) Cook for 4 to 5 minutes more or until pastry is golden brown. Remove from oven; set on a wire rack.

Reduce **Convection Roast** temperature to **300°F**. (Reduce standard oven temperature to 325°F.) Meanwhile, for filling, stir together eggs, milk, green onions, salt, pepper, and nutmeg. Stir in crab. Toss cheese and flour. Stir into egg mixture. Set the pastry shell on oven rack. Carefully pour filling into shell.

Convection Roast for 35 to 40 minutes or until a knife inserted near center comes out clean. (Or, standard bake for 35 to 40 minutes. If necessary, cover edge with foil the last 20 minutes to prevent over-browning.) Let stand for 10 minutes before serving.
Makes 8 appetizer servings.

Cheese and Olive Puff Ring

This irresistible hors d'oeuvre is a piquant version of cream puffs.

¾ cup water
6 tablespoons butter or margarine
⅛ teaspoon salt
¾ cup all-purpose flour
3 eggs
1 cup shredded Monterey Jack cheese with peppers (4 ounces)*
½ cup chopped, pitted ripe olives or pimiento-stuffed green olives
¼ cup grated Parmesan cheese
2 tablespoons grated Parmesan cheese

In a medium saucepan combine water, butter, and salt. Bring to boiling. Add flour all at once, stirring vigorously. Cook and stir until mixture forms a ball that doesn't separate. Remove from heat. Cool 5 minutes.

Add eggs, 1 at a time, beating with a spoon after each addition until smooth. Stir in Monterey Jack cheese, olives, and the ¼ cup Parmesan cheese.

Lightly grease and flour a 12-inch pizza pan or a baking sheet. Using a plate or lid as a guide, mark an 8-inch circle on the floured pan. Spoon the dough into 12 equal mounds onto the circle. Sprinkle with the 2 tablespoons Parmesan cheese.

Convection Bake in a preheated **375°F** oven about 35 minutes or until puffed, firm, and brown. (Or, standard bake in a preheated 400°F oven for 35 to 40 minutes.) Serve warm. Pull puffs apart for serving.
Makes 12 appetizer servings.

*Note: If desired, substitute shredded *mozzarella cheese* and 2 tablespoons canned diced *green chili peppers*, drained, for the Monterey Jack cheese with peppers.

Cheese-Stuffed Chicken in Phyllo

Dazzle your guests with this Greek-style entrée. They'll think you spent all day in the kitchen—but you didn't!

8	skinless, boneless chicken breast halves (about 2 pounds total)
	Salt
	Pepper
2	medium onions, chopped (about 1 cup)
2	tablespoons olive oil or cooking oil
1	10-ounce package frozen chopped spinach, thawed and well drained
4	ounces cream cheese, cubed and softened
1	cup shredded mozzarella cheese (4 ounces)
½	cup crumbled feta cheese (2 ounces)
½	cup shredded cheddar cheese (2 ounces)
1	egg yolk, beaten
1	tablespoon all-purpose flour
½	teaspoon ground nutmeg
½	teaspoon ground cumin
16	sheets frozen phyllo dough (18x14-inch rectangles), thawed
⅔	cup butter or margarine

Place each chicken breast between 2 sheets of heavy plastic wrap. Pound with the flat side of a meat mallet to ⅛-inch thickness. Remove plastic wrap. Sprinkle chicken with salt and pepper; set aside.

In a large skillet cook onions in oil until tender. Remove from heat. Stir in spinach. Stir in cream cheese until blended. Stir in mozzarella cheese, feta cheese, cheddar cheese, egg yolk, flour, nutmeg, and cumin.

Place about ⅓ cup of the spinach mixture on each chicken piece. Roll up chicken jelly-roll style (it's not necessary to seal ends).

Melt butter. Set aside 2 tablespoons of the melted butter. For each phyllo roll place a sheet of phyllo on work surface (keep remaining sheets covered with a damp towel to prevent drying out). Brush phyllo with some of the melted butter. Place another phyllo sheet on top of the first, then brush with butter. Place a chicken roll near a short side of the phyllo. Roll chicken and phyllo over once to enclose chicken. Fold in long sides of phyllo; continue rolling from short side. Repeat with the remaining chicken and phyllo sheets.

Place phyllo rolls in 2 large, shallow baking pans so rolls do not touch. Brush phyllo rolls with the reserved butter.

Convection Roast in a preheated **350°F** oven for 20 to 25 minutes or until chicken is tender and no longer pink. (Or, standard bake in a preheated 350°F oven for 30 to 35 minutes.)

Makes 8 main-dish servings.

Indian-Style Cornish Hens

Indian-Style Cornish Hens

A blend of seven seasonings gives these golden birds their extraordinary flavor.

- 2 teaspoons grated fresh gingerroot or ½ teaspoon ground ginger
- 2 cloves garlic, minced, or ¼ teaspoon garlic powder
- ¾ teaspoon ground cardamom
- ½ teaspoon fennel seed, crushed
- ¼ teaspoon ground cinnamon
- ¼ teaspoon ground red pepper
- ⅛ teaspoon ground cloves
- 2 Cornish game hens (1 to 1½ pounds each)
- 1 teaspoon cooking oil
  Hot cooked rice
  Orange wedges (optional)
  Celery leaves (optional)

In a small bowl combine ginger, garlic, cardamom, fennel seed, cinnamon, red pepper, and cloves.

Rinse game hens; pat dry with paper towels. Fasten neck skin to back of each hen with a small skewer. Use string to tie drumsticks to tail. Twist wing tips under back. Brush with cooking oil.

Cut small, deep slits all over hens. Rub with spice mixture, working mixture into slits. Cover and marinate in the refrigerator for 2 to 24 hours.

Place hens, breast sides up, on convection roasting rack set on top of broiler pan.

Convection Roast in a **350°F** oven for 50 to 65 minutes or until drumsticks move easily and juices run clear. (Or, standard roast in a 375°F oven for 1 to 1¼ hours. Cover hens loosely with foil during the first 45 minutes.)

Cover hens with foil and let stand for 10 minutes before carving. Serve with rice. If desired, garnish with oranges and celery. ***Makes 4 main-dish servings.***

Apricot-Glazed Duckling

- 1 4- to 5-pound domestic duckling
- ½ teaspoon dried oregano, crushed
- ¼ teaspoon onion salt
- ¼ teaspoon garlic salt
- ¼ teaspoon pepper
- ⅓ cup apricot preserves
- 2 tablespoons honey
- ½ teaspoon finely shredded lemon peel (set aside)
- 2 tablespoons lemon juice
- ½ cup chicken broth
- 2 teaspoons cornstarch
- 2 teaspoons soy sauce

Rinse duck; pat dry. Mix oregano, onion salt, garlic salt, and pepper. Sprinkle some of the mixture in cavity of duck; rub remaining mixture on skin.

Fasten neck skin to back with a small skewer. Tie drumsticks to tail. Twist wing tips under back. Prick skin with a fork.

Place duck, breast side up, on convection roasting rack set on top of broiler pan. Insert meat probe or a meat thermometer into center of an inside thigh muscle without touching bone.

Convection Roast in a **350°F** oven for 1¼ to 1½ hours or until probe registers 180°F to 185°F. (Or, standard roast in a 375°F oven for 1¾ to 2¼ hours.) After 45 minutes, cut string between drumsticks.

Meanwhile, for glaze, combine apricot preserves, honey, and lemon juice. Cook and stir just until melted. Baste duck with *half* of the glaze during the last 5 to 10 minutes of roasting. Cover duck with foil and let stand for 15 minutes before carving.

For sauce, combine chicken broth and cornstarch. Stir into the remaining glaze. Stir in lemon peel and soy sauce. Cook and stir until thickened and bubbly. Cook and stir for 1 to 2 minutes more. Serve sauce with duck. ***Makes 4 main-dish servings.***

Red Snapper with Tomatoes and Feta Cheese

This sublime flavor combination also enhances whitefish, rockfish, or lake trout.

- 1 pound fresh or frozen red snapper fillets, ½ to ¾ inch thick
- 1 14½-ounce can tomatoes, cut up
- 4 green onions, sliced (about ½ cup)
- ¼ cup thinly sliced celery
- 2 tablespoons lemon juice
- 1 teaspoon dried oregano, crushed
- ¼ teaspoon pepper
- ¼ teaspoon ground coriander
- ¼ cup crumbled feta cheese (1 ounce)
- 2 tablespoons sliced, pitted ripe olives
  Parsley sprigs (optional)

Thaw fish, if frozen.

For sauce, in a large skillet combine *undrained* tomatoes, green onions, celery, lemon juice, and oregano; bring to boiling. Reduce heat and simmer, uncovered, about 15 minutes or until most of the liquid is evaporated.

Meanwhile, cut fish into 4 serving-size pieces. Place fish in a greased, 2-quart rectangular baking dish, tucking under any thin edges so fish is a uniform thickness. Sprinkle with pepper and coriander.

Convection Bake in a preheated **425°F** oven until fish just begins to flake easily with a fork. Allow 4 to 6 minutes per ½-inch thickness. (Or, standard bake in a preheated 450°F oven. Allow 4 to 6 minutes per ½-inch thickness.)

To serve, transfer fish to dinner plates. Spoon sauce over fish. Sprinkle with cheese and olives. If desired, garnish with parsley.
Makes 4 main-dish servings.

Bacon-Stuffed Flounder Rolls

Delicate flounder makes a wonderful wrapper for the flavorful bacon-and-herb stuffing.

- 3 slices bacon
  Butter or margarine, melted
- 2 cups herb-seasoned stuffing mix
- ⅓ cup water
- 1 small onion, finely chopped (about ¼ cup)
- 2 tablespoons snipped parsley
- 6 4-ounce skinless flounder or sole fillets
- 1 tablespoon butter or margarine, melted
- 2 tablespoons butter or margarine
- 2 tablespoons all-purpose flour
- 1¼ cups milk
- 1 cup shredded cheddar cheese (4 ounces)

For stuffing, cook bacon until crisp. Drain, reserving the drippings. Crumble bacon; set aside. Measure drippings; add enough melted butter to equal ¼ cup. Combine stuffing mix, water, onion, and the drippings mixture. Stir in bacon and parsley.

Divide stuffing into 6 portions and form into balls. Place a ball of stuffing on top of each fish fillet and roll up. Secure with wooden toothpicks. Place fish rolls, seam sides down, in a greased, 2-quart rectangular baking dish. Brush with the 1 tablespoon melted butter.

Convection Bake in a preheated **350°F** oven for 18 to 20 minutes or until fish just begins to flake easily with a fork. (Or, standard bake in a preheated 375°F oven about 20 minutes.)

Meanwhile, for sauce, in a small saucepan melt the 2 tablespoons butter. Stir in flour. Add milk all at once. Cook and stir until thickened and bubbly. Cook and stir for 1 minute more. Add cheese; stir until melted.

To serve, transfer fish rolls to a platter. Remove toothpicks. Spoon sauce over fish rolls.
Makes 6 main-dish servings.

Calypso Pork

The savory seasonings add a lot of flavor and give the roast a rich, dark color.

- 3 green onions, sliced (about ⅓ cup)
- 1 tablespoon soy sauce
- 2 teaspoons cooking oil
- ½ teaspoon salt
- ½ teaspoon ground ginger
- ½ teaspoon ground allspice
- ¼ teaspoon ground red pepper
- ¼ teaspoon ground cinnamon
- ¼ teaspoon ground nutmeg
- 1 3- to 4-pound boneless pork top loin roast (double loin, tied)
- 2 tablespoons cornstarch
- 1½ cups unsweetened pineapple juice

In a blender container or food processor bowl mix onions, soy, oil, salt, ginger, allspice, red pepper, cinnamon, and nutmeg. Cover and blend or process until nearly smooth.

Remove string or netting from meat. Trim fat; separate meat. Pat soy mixture onto all sides of meat. Reassemble meat; tie with clean cotton string. Cover and marinate in refrigerator for 8 to 24 hours.

Place meat on convection roasting rack set on top of broiler pan. Insert meat probe or a meat thermometer into center of the meat.

Convection Roast in a **325°F** oven 1½ to 2¼ hours or until probe registers 155°F. (Or, standard roast in a 325°F oven for 1¾ to 2½ hours.) Remove from pan, reserving ¼ *cup* of the drippings. Cover meat with foil; let stand 15 minutes before carving. (Temperature will rise during standing time.)

Meanwhile, in a small saucepan combine the reserved drippings and the cornstarch. Add pineapple juice all at once. Cook and stir until thickened and bubbly. Cook and stir for 2 minutes more. Serve with meat.
Makes 8 to 10 main-dish servings.

Pork Medaillons with Brandy-Cream Sauce

Team this company-pleasing pork entrée with a spinach salad, steamed baby carrots, and crusty Baguettes (see recipe, page 61).

- 1 2- to 2½-pound boneless pork top loin roast (single loin)
  Pepper
- ⅓ cup chicken broth
- 1 tablespoon chopped shallot or green onion
- ¼ cup whipping cream
- ¼ cup brandy or chicken broth
- ½ cup unsalted butter, cut into small pieces and softened
- 1 teaspoon lemon juice
- ¼ teaspoon salt
- ⅛ teaspoon white pepper

Trim fat from meat. Rub meat with pepper. Place meat on convection roasting rack set on top of broiler pan. Insert meat probe or a meat thermometer into center of the meat.

Convection Roast in a **325°F** oven for 1 to 1¼ hours or until probe registers 155°F. (Or, standard roast in a 325°F oven for 1 to 1¼ hours.) Cover meat with foil and let stand for 10 minutes before carving. (Temperature will rise during standing time.)

Meanwhile, for sauce, in a medium saucepan combine the ⅓ cup chicken broth and the shallot; bring to boiling. Reduce heat, cover, and simmer for 2 minutes. Stir in whipping cream and brandy. Cook, uncovered, over medium heat about 10 minutes or until sauce is reduced to ⅓ cup. Remove from heat. Strain sauce; return sauce to pan.

Add butter to sauce, 1 piece at a time, stirring constantly with a wire whisk. Stir in lemon juice, salt, and white pepper.

Slice meat and serve with sauce.
Makes 6 main-dish servings.

Roast Lamb with Rosemary-Lemon Sauce

Roast Lamb with Rosemary-Lemon Sauce

Delight guests by serving this sophisticated roast with rice pilaf, asparagus, and Raspberry-Pear Pie (see recipe, page 80).

- 1 1¼- to 1½-pound lamb rib roast, backbone loosened
- 1 teaspoon snipped fresh rosemary or ¼ teaspoon dried rosemary, crushed
- 2 cloves garlic, minced
    Salt and pepper
- ⅔ cup beef broth
- ½ teaspoon finely shredded lemon peel
- 1 tablespoon lemon juice
- 2 teaspoons cornstarch
- 1 teaspoon honey
- ⅛ teaspoon pepper
    Thin strips of lemon peel (optional)

Trim fat from meat. Rub meat with *half* of the rosemary and all of the garlic. Sprinkle with salt and pepper.

Place meat, rib side down, on convection roasting rack set on top of broiler pan. Insert meat probe or a meat thermometer into the center of the meat without touching bone.

Convection Roast in a **400°F** oven about 30 minutes for medium-rare or until probe registers 140°F. (Or, standard roast in a 400°F oven for 30 to 35 minutes.) Cover with foil and let stand for 10 to 15 minutes before carving. (Temperature will rise during standing time.)

Meanwhile, for sauce, in a small saucepan stir together broth, shredded lemon peel, lemon juice, cornstarch, honey, pepper, and the remaining rosemary. Cook and stir until thickened and bubbly. Cook and stir for 2 minutes more. To serve, slice meat between ribs and top with sauce. If desired, garnish with strips of lemon peel.
Makes 4 main-dish servings.

Marinated Prime Rib

Ask your butcher to cut a roast from the small end of the rack of ribs. A smaller-diameter roast will absorb more of the tangy marinade flavor.

- ¾ cup dry red wine
- 1 medium onion, chopped (about ½ cup)
- ¼ cup lemon juice
- ¼ cup water
- 1 tablespoon Worcestershire sauce
- ½ teaspoon dried rosemary, crushed
- ½ teaspoon dried marjoram, crushed
- ¼ teaspoon garlic salt
- 1 4- to 5-pound beef rib roast (from small end)

For marinade, in a small bowl combine red wine, onion, lemon juice, water, Worcestershire sauce, rosemary, marjoram, and garlic salt.

Place meat in a large plastic bag set in a shallow dish. Add marinade; close bag. Marinate in the refrigerator for 6 to 24 hours, turning bag occasionally.

Drain meat, discarding marinade. Place meat, fat side up, on convection roasting rack set on top of broiler pan. Insert meat probe or a meat thermometer into the center of the meat without touching bone.

Convection Roast in a **325°F** oven for 1¾ to 2 hours for medium-rare (140°F) or 2 to 2½ hours for medium (155°F). (Or, standard roast in a 325°F oven for 1¾ to 2¼ hours for medium-rare [140°F] or 2¼ to 2¾ hours for medium [155°F].) Cover with foil and let stand for 15 minutes before carving. (Temperature will rise during standing time.) To serve, slice meat.
Makes 10 to 12 main-dish servings.

Chocolate Chip Tart

Invite friends over after a show or concert and serve this decadent tart with flavored coffee.

Pastry for Single-Crust Pie (see recipe, page 81)
3 eggs
1 cup light corn syrup
½ cup packed brown sugar
⅓ cup butter or margarine, melted and cooled
1 teaspoon vanilla
1 cup coarsely chopped, lightly salted mixed nuts
½ cup miniature semisweet chocolate pieces
¼ cup fudge ice-cream topping

Prepare Pastry for Single-Crust Pie. On a lightly floured surface, roll dough into a 12-inch circle. Fit pastry into an 11-inch round tart pan with a removable bottom. Trim pastry even with rim of pan.

For filling, in a large mixing bowl use a rotary beater or wire whisk to lightly beat eggs just until mixed. Stir in corn syrup. Add brown sugar, melted butter, and vanilla, stirring until sugar is dissolved. Stir in nuts and chocolate pieces.

Set pastry-lined tart pan on the oven rack. Carefully pour filling into tart pan.

Convection Roast in a preheated **325°F** oven for 30 to 35 minutes or until a knife inserted near the center comes out clean. (Or, standard bake in a preheated 350°F oven about 40 minutes.) Cool on wire rack.

To serve, remove sides from pan. Cut tart into wedges and transfer to dessert plates. In a small saucepan heat and stir ice-cream topping over medium heat just until heated through. Cool slightly. Drizzle in zigzag lines across each piece of tart, overlapping onto plate. Cover tart and refrigerate to store.
Makes 8 to 10 servings.

Strudel Sticks

Your guests will find it hard to settle for just one of these feather-light pastries.

6 ounces cream cheese, softened
⅓ cup granulated sugar
2 teaspoons poppy seeds
2 sheets frozen puff pastry (one 17¼-ounce package), thawed
Sliced almonds, poppy seeds, or coarse sugar (optional)

For filling, in a small bowl combine cream cheese, sugar, and the 2 teaspoons poppy seeds. Set aside.

On a lightly floured surface, unfold pastry. Cut each sheet into six 5x3-inch rectangles.

Brush edges of pastry rectangles with a little water. Place about 1 tablespoon of the filling in the center of each rectangle; spread to ½ inch from edges. Starting from a long side, roll up pastry jelly-roll style. Pinch edges and seams to seal. If desired, lightly brush tops with water and sprinkle with almonds. Place, seam sides down, on a lightly greased baking sheet.

Convection Roast in a preheated **350°F** oven for 15 to 18 minutes or until deep golden brown. (Or, standard bake in a preheated 350°F oven for 20 to 25 minutes.) Serve strudel warm or cool.
Makes 12 servings.

Pecan Cake with Tangerine Cream Filling

Celebrate a special birthday or anniversary with this scrumptious nut torte.

2½	cups broken pecans, toasted (see tip, page 69)
3	tablespoons all-purpose flour
4	teaspoons baking powder
6	eggs
1	cup granulated sugar
1	8-ounce package cream cheese, softened
¼	cup butter or margarine
½	cup packed brown sugar
1¾	teaspoons finely shredded tangerine peel or orange peel, divided
1	teaspoon vanilla
1½	cups whipping cream
2	tablespoons granulated sugar

In a blender container or food processor bowl place *half* of the pecans. Cover and blend or process until coarsely ground. Remove and set aside. Repeat with remaining pecans.

In a small bowl combine ground pecans, flour, and baking powder. In blender container or food processor bowl place eggs and the 1 cup granulated sugar. Cover and blend or process until smooth. Add pecan mixture. Cover and blend or process until smooth, stopping and scraping sides as needed to mix evenly. (Mixture may be foamy.) Spread in 2 greased and lightly floured 8x1½-inch round baking pans.

Convection Bake in a preheated **325°F** oven about 25 minutes or until lightly browned and tops spring back when lightly touched. (Centers may dip slightly.) (Or, standard bake in a preheated 350°F oven for 25 to 30 minutes.) Cool in pans on wire racks for 10 minutes. Remove from pans. Cool completely on wire racks.

For filling, in a small mixing bowl beat cream cheese and butter with an electric mixer on medium-high speed until fluffy. Gradually add brown sugar, beating for 3 to 4 minutes or until smooth. Stir in *1 teaspoon* of the tangerine peel and the vanilla.

To assemble, using a serrated knife, cut cake layers in half horizontally (4 layers total). Place a split cake layer, cut side up, on a platter. Spread about *½ cup* of the filling on top of cake layer. Place another split layer, cut side down, on top of filling. Spread layer with another *½ cup* of the filling. Repeat with the remaining split cake layers and filling, ending with a cake layer on top.

In a chilled small mixing bowl combine whipping cream, the 2 tablespoons sugar, and the remaining tangerine peel. Beat with chilled beaters on medium speed until soft peaks form (tips curl). Frost top and sides of cake with whipped cream. Cover and refrigerate for up to 4 hours to store.
Makes 12 servings.

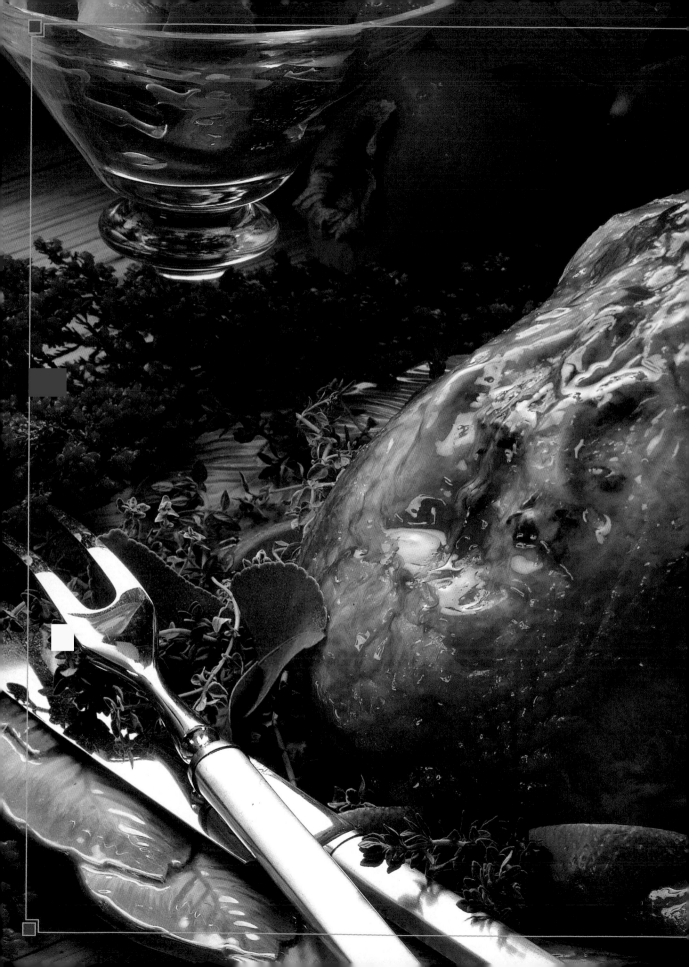

Tempting Entrées

You'll please everyone around your dinner table with these sumptuous recipes flawlessly cooked in your convection oven. You'll find something here for every meal of the week, from beautifully browned Chicken Potpies with Cheddar Pastry to golden Honey-Herb Roast Chicken with herbs cooked under the crisp skin.

Honey-Herb Roast Chicken (see recipe, page 24)

Honey-Herb Roast Chicken

Once you've sampled this tasty soy-honey glaze, you'll never settle for plain roast chicken again. (Pictured on pages 22–23.)

- 2 tablespoons honey
- 1 tablespoon soy sauce
- 1 tablespoon lime juice
- 1 2½- to 3-pound broiler-fryer chicken
  Salt
  Pepper
- 2 teaspoons snipped fresh thyme or
    ½ teaspoon dried thyme, crushed
- 2 cloves garlic, thinly sliced
  Lime wedges (optional)
  Fresh thyme sprigs (optional)

For glaze, in a small bowl combine honey, soy sauce, and lime juice; set aside.

Rinse chicken; pat dry with paper towels. Sprinkle body cavity with salt and pepper.

Slip your fingers under the skin of the chicken to loosen skin from breast. Place snipped thyme and garlic between skin and chicken breast.

Fasten neck skin to back of chicken with a small skewer. Use string to tie drumsticks to tail. Twist wing tips under back. Place the chicken, breast side up, on convection roasting rack set on top of broiler pan.

Convection Roast in a **350°F** oven for 50 to 65 minutes or until drumsticks move easily and juices run clear. (Or, standard roast in a 375°F oven for 1 to 1¼ hours.) Cut string between drumsticks and brush chicken twice with the glaze during the last 5 to 10 minutes of roasting.

Cover chicken with foil and let stand for 10 minutes before carving. Transfer chicken to a platter. If desired, garnish with lime wedges and fresh thyme sprigs.
Makes 4 to 6 servings.

Using the Meat Probe or a Meat Thermometer

To roast meat or poultry in your *KitchenAid®* convection oven just the way you like it, use the probe provided with your oven or use a meat thermometer.

Start by inserting the probe or thermometer into the center of the largest muscle or thickest portion of the meat or poultry, making sure the thermometer does not touch fat or bone, or the bottom of the pan.

Roast until the probe or thermometer registers the degree of doneness you've chosen. When the probe temperature is reached, the oven will automatically shut off. Use the temperatures listed in the recipe or in the Roasting Meats and Poultry chart on page 29.

If using a thermometer, remove meat or poultry from the oven when it has reached the desired internal temperature.

To carve the meat or poultry easily, cover it and let it stand for 10 to 15 minutes before slicing. The temperature will continue to rise as the meat or poultry stands.

Pesto-Stuffed Turkey Breast

Try this sophisticated dish when your holiday plans call for a small dinner gathering.

- ½ cup firmly packed torn fresh spinach leaves
- ¼ cup firmly packed fresh basil leaves or parsley leaves
- ¼ cup grated Parmesan cheese
- 2 tablespoons chopped walnuts, toasted (see tip, page 69)
- 1 small clove garlic, quartered
- 2 tablespoons olive oil or cooking oil
- 1 2½- to 3-pound fresh turkey breast half

For pesto, in a blender container or food processor bowl combine spinach, basil, Parmesan cheese, walnuts, and garlic. Cover and blend or process with several on-off pulses until a paste forms, stopping and scraping the sides as necessary.

With the blender or processor running slowly, gradually add oil and blend or process until the pesto is the consistency of soft butter. Set pesto aside.

Rinse turkey; pat dry with paper towels. Slip your fingers under the skin of the turkey to loosen skin, leaving it attached at a long edge. Spread the pesto over the meat, under the skin. Fold the skin over pesto; fasten with wooden toothpicks.

Place turkey, skin side up, on convection roasting rack set on top of broiler pan. Insert meat probe or a meat thermometer into the thickest portion of the turkey.

Convection Roast in a **325°F** oven for 1¼ to 1½ hours or until meat probe registers 170°F. (Or, standard roast in a 325°F oven for 1¼ to 1½ hours.) Cover with foil and let stand 10 minutes before carving.
Makes 6 to 8 servings.

Herb and Pecan Oven-Fried Chicken

Crisp fried chicken is easy to prepare and lower in fat with this convection oven method.

- 4 large chicken breast halves with bones (2 to 2½ pounds total)
- 1 egg
- 1 tablespoon milk
- ¾ cup herb-seasoned stuffing mix, slightly crushed
- ⅓ cup finely chopped pecans
- 2 tablespoons snipped parsley
- 1 tablespoon snipped fresh basil or ½ teaspoon dried basil, crushed
- ⅛ teaspoon onion powder
  Dash pepper

If desired, skin chicken. Rinse chicken; pat dry with paper towels.

In a shallow bowl or pie plate stir together egg and milk. In another shallow bowl combine stuffing mix, pecans, parsley, basil, onion powder, and pepper.

Dip chicken into egg mixture. Coat with pecan mixture. Place chicken, meaty side up, in a 13x9x2-inch baking pan.

Convection Bake in a preheated **375°F** oven for 30 to 35 minutes or until chicken is tender and no longer pink. (Or, standard bake in a preheated 375°F oven for 45 to 55 minutes.)
Makes 4 servings.

Chicken with Cherry Sauce

Chicken with Cherry Sauce

Cherries and chicken are a spectacular duo! Look for dried cherries near the raisins or in the produce section of your supermarket.

- 4 skinless, boneless chicken breast halves (about 1 pound total)
   Ground nutmeg
   Salt
   Pepper
- 2 teaspoons cornstarch
- 1 teaspoon brown sugar
   Dash pepper
- ½ cup unsweetened pineapple juice
- ⅓ cup chicken broth
- ¼ cup dried cherries or golden raisins, coarsely chopped

Preheat on **Convection Broil** at **450°F** for 5 minutes. (Or, preheat standard broiler.) Meanwhile, rinse chicken; pat dry with paper towels. Sprinkle lightly with nutmeg, salt, and pepper.

Place chicken, boned side up, on the unheated broiler pan.

Convection Broil for 7 to 10 minutes or until chicken is tender and no longer pink, turning once. (Or, standard broil 4 to 5 inches from the heat for 12 to 15 minutes, turning once.)

Meanwhile, for sauce, in a small saucepan combine cornstarch, brown sugar, and pepper; stir in pineapple juice and chicken broth. Cook and stir over medium heat until thickened and bubbly.

Stir in cherries. Cook and stir 2 minutes more. Serve sauce with chicken.

Makes 4 servings.

Curry-Cajun Spiced Chicken

Cajun seasoning is a mixture of salt, ground red pepper, garlic, and other spices typical of the cooking of southern Louisiana.

- 6 skinless, boneless chicken breast halves (about 1½ pounds total)
- ⅓ cup honey
- 3 tablespoons prepared mustard
- 3 tablespoons water
- 2 tablespoons butter or margarine, melted
- 2 to 3 teaspoons Cajun seasoning
- 2 to 3 teaspoons curry powder
- 1 teaspoon lemon juice
- 1 clove garlic, minced
   Hot cooked rice

Rinse chicken; pat dry with paper towels. In a 3-quart rectangular baking dish combine honey, mustard, water, melted butter, Cajun seasoning, curry powder, lemon juice, and garlic; mix well. Add chicken, turning to coat with butter mixture.

Convection Bake in a **325°F** oven for 20 to 25 minutes or until chicken is tender and no longer pink. (Or, standard bake in a 350°F oven about 30 minutes.) Serve chicken with pan juices and rice.

Makes 6 servings.

Chicken Potpies with Cheddar Pastry

These bubbly chicken and vegetable pies are comfort food designed for today's taste.

- 1½ cups chicken broth, divided
- 1 large onion, chopped (about 1 cup)
- 1 stalk celery, chopped (about ½ cup)
- 1 medium carrot, sliced (about ½ cup)
- ¼ cup all-purpose flour
- ½ teaspoon dried sage, crushed
- ¼ teaspoon salt
- ¼ teaspoon garlic powder
- ⅛ teaspoon pepper
- ½ cup tomato sauce
- 2 cups chopped cooked chicken or turkey
- 2 tablespoons snipped parsley
  Cheddar Pastry (see recipe at right)
  Milk

In a large saucepan combine *1 cup* of the chicken broth, the onion, celery, and carrot; bring to boiling. Reduce heat, cover, and simmer for 5 to 7 minutes or until vegetables are tender-crisp.

In a small bowl combine the remaining ½ cup chicken broth, the flour, sage, salt, garlic powder, and pepper. Stir into the vegetable mixture. Add tomato sauce. Cook and stir until thickened and bubbly. Stir in chicken and parsley; heat through.

Prepare Cheddar Pastry. Divide dough into 4 portions. Form each portion into a ball. On a lightly floured surface, roll a portion of dough into a circle 1 inch wider than a 12- to 14-ounce casserole. Repeat with the remaining dough to make 4 pastry rounds.

Divide the chicken mixture evenly among four 12- to 14-ounce casseroles. Place a pastry round on top of each casserole. Flute to edges of dishes. Brush tops with milk.

Convection Roast in a preheated **400°F** oven for 15 to 20 minutes or until pastry is golden brown. (Or, standard bake in a preheated 425°F oven about 25 minutes.) *Makes 4 servings.*

Cheddar Pastry

For a favorite combination of fruit and cheese, use this pastry for a crumb-topped apple pie.

- 1½ cups all-purpose flour
- ⅓ cup shredded cheddar cheese (1½ ounces)
- ⅛ teaspoon salt
- ½ cup shortening
- 4 to 5 tablespoons cold water

In a medium bowl stir together flour, cheddar cheese, and salt. Using a pastry blender, cut in shortening until the pieces are the size of small peas.

Sprinkle cold water, 1 tablespoon at a time, over mixture, tossing with a fork after each addition until all is moistened. Form dough into a ball.

Continue as directed for Chicken Potpies. Or, for a single-crust pie, on a lightly floured surface flatten ball of dough. Roll dough into a 12-inch circle. Fit pastry into a 9-inch pie plate, being careful not to stretch pastry. *Makes one 9-inch single-crust pastry.*

Roasting Meats and Poultry

Place meat or poultry on the convection roasting rack set on top of the broiler pan. (Or, for standard roasting, place on a rack in a shallow roasting pan.) Insert meat probe or a meat thermometer. Starting in an unheated oven, **Convection Roast** (or standard roast) at the oven temperature and for the time given or until probe or thermometer registers the specified temperature. Cover with foil and let stand for 10 to 20 minutes before carving. The temperature will rise during standing time.

	Oven Temp.	Time	Doneness
Beef			
Beef rib roast, from small end (4 to 5 pounds)			
Convection	325°F	1¾ to 2 hours	medium-rare 140°F
	325°F	2 to 2½ hours	medium 155°F
Standard	325°F	1¾ to 2¼ hours	medium-rare 140°F
	325°F	2¼ to 2¾ hours	medium 155°F
Beef rib eye roast (4 to 4½ pounds)			
Convection	350°F	1¼ to 1¾ hours	medium-rare 140°F
	350°F	1½ to 2 hours	medium 155°F
Standard	350°F	1¼ to 1¾ hours	medium-rare 140°F
	350°F	1½ to 2 hours	medium 155°F
Beef sirloin roast, boneless (4 to 5 pounds)			
Convection	325°F	1½ to 2 hours	medium-rare 140°F
	325°F	2 to 2½ hours	medium 155°F
Standard	325°F	2¼ to 2¾ hours	medium-rare 140°F
	325°F	2¾ to 3¼ hours	medium 155°F
Pork			
Pork top loin roast (single loin), boneless (2 to 2½ pounds)			
Convection	325°F	1 to 1¼ hours	155°F
Standard	325°F	1 to 1¼ hours	155°F
Pork top loin roast (double loin, tied), boneless (3 to 4 pounds)			
Convection	325°F	1½ to 2¼ hours	155°F
Standard	325°F	1¾ to 2½ hours	155°F
Pork loin center rib roast (3 to 4 pounds)			
Convection	325°F	1¼ to 1¾ hours	155°F
Standard	325°F	1½ to 2 hours	155°F
Ham			
Ham, fully cooked shank half (4 to 5 pounds)			
Convection	300°F	1½ to 2 hours	135°F
Standard	325°F	1½ to 2 hours	135°F

	Oven Temp.	Time	Doneness
Lamb			
Lamb rib roast (1¼ to 1½ pounds)			
Convection	400°F	30 minutes	140°F
Standard	400°F	30 to 35 minutes	140°F
Leg of Lamb (4 to 5 pounds)			
Convection	325°F	1¼ to 1½ hours	140°F
Standard	325°F	1¼ to 1¾ hours	140°F
Chicken*			
Chicken, broiler-fryer (2½ to 3 pounds)			
Convection	350°F	50 to 65 minutes	
Standard	375°F	1 to 1¼ hours	
Chicken, roasting (6 to 6½ pounds)			
Convection	300°F	1¾ to 2 hours	180°F to 185°F
Standard	325°F	2½ to 2¾ hours	180°F to 185°F
Turkey*			
Turkey (10 to 12 pounds)			
Convection	300°F	1¾ to 2¼ hours	180°F to 185°F
Standard	325°F	3½ to 4 hours	180°F to 185°F
Turkey (14 to 16 pounds)			
Convection	300°F	2¼ to 2¾ hours	180°F to 185°F
Standard	325°F	4½ to 5 hours	180°F to 185°F
Turkey breast half, fresh (2½ to 3 pounds)			
Convection	325°F	1¼ to 1½ hours	170°F
Standard	325°F	1¼ to 1½ hours	170°F
Cornish game hens*			
Cornish game hens (1 to 1½ pounds each)			
Convection	350°F	50 to 65 minutes	
Standard	375°F	1 to 1¼ hours	

***Note:** If convection roasting, *do not stuff* poultry.

Apricot-Stuffed Steaks

Apricot-Stuffed Steaks

These mouthwatering steaks are easy enough for special family meals and fancy enough for company dinners.

- 2 8-ounce beef top loin steaks, cut 1 to 1¼ inches thick
  Pepper
- 16 dried apricot halves, finely chopped
- 4 tablespoons sliced almonds, toasted (see tip, page 69)
- ⅔ cup apricot nectar or orange juice
- 1 green onion, thinly sliced (about 2 tablespoons)
- 1 teaspoon cornstarch
- 1 teaspoon instant chicken bouillon granules
- ⅛ teaspoon pepper

Trim fat from meat. Make a pocket in each steak by cutting a deep horizontal slit. Sprinkle pepper inside pockets. Using *half* of the apricots and *half* of the almonds, place in pockets. If necessary, fasten openings of pockets with wooden toothpicks.

Preheat on **Convection Broil** at **450°F** for 5 minutes. (Or, preheat standard broiler.) Place steaks on the unheated broiler pan.

Convection Broil to desired doneness, turning once. Allow 10 to 13 minutes for medium-rare, 12 to 15 minutes for medium, or 17 to 20 minutes for well-done. (Or, standard broil 3 to 4 inches from the heat, turning once. Allow 12 to 14 minutes for medium-rare or 14 to 16 minutes for medium.)

Meanwhile, for sauce, in a small saucepan combine apricot nectar, the remaining apricots, green onion, cornstarch, bouillon granules, and the ⅛ teaspoon pepper. Cook and stir until thickened and bubbly. Cook and stir for 1 minute more.

To serve, cut each steak in half. Transfer to dinner plates. Spoon the sauce over steaks. Sprinkle with the remaining almonds.
Makes 4 servings.

Dill and Onion Steaks

- ½ cup dry white wine
- 1 tablespoon olive oil or cooking oil
- 2½ teaspoons dried dillweed, divided
- 1⅛ teaspoons coarsely ground pepper, divided
- ½ teaspoon salt
- 8 4-ounce beef tenderloin steaks, cut 1 inch thick
- 2 large onions, thinly sliced and separated into rings (about 2 cups)
- ⅔ cup mayonnaise or salad dressing
- ⅓ cup dairy sour cream
- 4 teaspoons prepared horseradish
- ⅛ teaspoon salt

For marinade, in a small bowl combine wine, oil, *1½ teaspoons* of the dillweed, *1 teaspoon* of the pepper, and the ½ teaspoon salt.

Trim fat from meat. Place steaks and onions in a large plastic bag set in a shallow dish. Add marinade; close bag. Marinate in the refrigerator for 4 to 24 hours, turning bag occasionally. Drain steaks, reserving marinade and onions.

Preheat on **Convection Broil** at **450°F** for 5 minutes. (Or, preheat standard broiler.) Place steaks on the unheated broiler pan.

Convection Broil to desired doneness, turning once. Allow 10 to 12 minutes for medium-rare or 12 to 14 minutes for medium. (Or, standard broil 3 to 4 inches from the heat, turning once. Allow 12 to 14 minutes for medium-rare or 14 to 16 minutes for medium.) Meanwhile, in a large skillet heat the reserved marinade and onions to boiling. Reduce heat, cover, and simmer for 10 to 12 minutes or until onions are tender. For sauce, combine mayonnaise, sour cream, horseradish, the ⅛ teaspoon salt, the remaining 1 teaspoon dillweed, and the remaining ⅛ teaspoon pepper. Serve steaks with onion mixture and sauce.
Makes 8 servings.

Rib Eye Roast with Herb and Mushroom Sauce

 1 4- to 4½-pound beef rib eye roast (from small end)
 1 teaspoon lemon-pepper seasoning
 2 tablespoons butter or margarine
2½ ounces fresh mushrooms, sliced (about 1 cup)
 1 small onion, chopped (about ¼ cup)
 2 cloves garlic, minced
 ¼ teaspoon dried thyme, crushed
 2 tablespoons all-purpose flour
 1 cup light cream, half and half, or milk
 1 teaspoon instant beef bouillon granules
 2 tablespoons snipped parsley
 1 tablespoon brandy (optional)

Trim fat from meat. Moisten meat with water; rub with lemon-pepper seasoning. Place meat on convection roasting rack set on top of broiler pan. Insert meat probe or a meat thermometer into the thickest portion of meat.

Convection Roast in a **350°F** oven for 1¼ to 1¾ hours for medium-rare (140°F) or 1½ to 2 hours for medium (155°F). (Or, standard roast in a 350°F oven for 1¼ to 1¾ hours for medium-rare [140°F] or 1½ to 2 hours for medium [155°F].) Cover with foil and let stand for 15 minutes before carving. (Temperature will rise during standing time.)

Meanwhile, for sauce, in a medium saucepan melt butter. Add mushrooms, onion, garlic, and thyme. Cook over medium-high heat for 4 to 5 minutes or until onion is tender, stirring frequently. Stir in flour. Add cream and bouillon granules all at once. Cook and stir until thickened and bubbly. Add parsley and, if desired, brandy. Cook and stir for 1 minute more. If too thick, stir in a little additional cream and heat through.

To serve, slice meat and serve with sauce.
Makes 12 to 14 servings.

Spinach-Stuffed Meat Loaf

 2 eggs
 ¾ cup soft bread crumbs (about 1 slice)
 1 8-ounce can tomato sauce, divided
 1 medium onion, finely chopped (about ½ cup), divided
 1 small green pepper, finely chopped (about ½ cup), divided
 ½ teaspoon garlic salt
 ¼ teaspoon pepper
1½ pounds lean ground beef
 5 ounces frozen chopped spinach, thawed and well drained
 ½ cup ricotta cheese
 2 tablespoons grated Parmesan cheese
 1 teaspoon dried basil or marjoram, crushed
 1 7½-ounce can tomatoes, cut up
 1 small carrot, shredded (about ⅓ cup)
 1 teaspoon granulated sugar
 1 clove garlic, minced
 ⅛ teaspoon pepper

Separate *1* of the eggs, reserving the egg white. Combine egg yolk, whole egg, bread crumbs, ¼ cup of the tomato sauce, ¼ cup of the onion, ¼ cup of the green pepper, the garlic salt, and the ¼ teaspoon pepper. Add meat; mix well. Combine the reserved egg white, spinach, cheeses, and ½ *teaspoon* of the basil. Pat *half* of the meat mixture into a 9x5x3-inch loaf pan. Top with spinach mixture, then the remaining meat mixture.

Convection Bake in a **325°F** oven for 50 to 55 minutes or until no pink remains. (Or, standard bake in a 350°F oven for 1 to 1¼ hours.) Meanwhile, for sauce, combine reserved tomato sauce, the remaining ¼ cup onion, the remaining ¼ cup green pepper, the remaining ½ teaspoon basil, *undrained* tomatoes, carrot, sugar, garlic, and the ⅛ teaspoon pepper. Cover and simmer for 10 minutes. Let meat loaf stand for 5 minutes before serving. Serve with sauce.
Makes 6 servings.

Pastitsio

Oregano and cinnamon give this traditional Greek dish its irresistible flavor.

- 1 cup elbow macaroni
- 1 pound ground lamb, beef, or pork
- 1 medium onion, chopped (about ½ cup)
- 2 cloves garlic, minced
- 1 8-ounce can tomato sauce
- ¼ cup dry red wine or beef broth
- 2 tablespoons snipped parsley
- ½ teaspoon dried oregano, crushed
- ¼ teaspoon salt
- ¼ teaspoon ground cinnamon
- 4 eggs, divided
- 3 tablespoons butter or margarine
- 3 tablespoons all-purpose flour
- ¼ teaspoon pepper
- 1¾ cups milk, divided
- ½ cup grated Parmesan cheese, divided
  Ground cinnamon (optional)

Cook the macaroni according to package directions; drain. Meanwhile, in a large skillet cook meat, onion, and garlic until meat is brown and onion is tender. Drain off fat. Stir in tomato sauce, wine, parsley, oregano, salt, and the ¼ teaspoon cinnamon. Bring to boiling. Reduce heat and simmer, uncovered, for 10 minutes. Gradually stir meat mixture into *1* of the beaten eggs; set meat mixture aside.

For sauce, in a medium saucepan melt butter. Stir in flour and pepper. Add *1½ cups* of the milk all at once. Cook and stir until thickened and bubbly. Cook and stir for 1 minute more. In a medium bowl beat *2* of the eggs. Gradually stir sauce into eggs. Stir in *¼ cup* of the Parmesan cheese.

In a large bowl toss together the cooked macaroni, the remaining beaten egg, the remaining ¼ cup Parmesan cheese, and the remaining ¼ cup milk.

To assemble, in a 2-quart square baking dish layer *half* of the macaroni mixture, all of the meat mixture, the remaining macaroni mixture, and all of the sauce. If desired, sprinkle with additional cinnamon.

Convection Bake in a preheated **325°F** oven about 30 minutes or until set. (Or, standard bake in a preheated 350°F oven for 30 to 35 minutes.) Let stand for 5 minutes before serving.
Makes 6 servings.

Pork Chops with Currant-Nut Stuffing

Pork Chops with Currant-Nut Stuffing

For a festive touch, garnish the chops with sprigs of sage and fresh raspberries.

- 4 pork loin rib chops, cut 1¼ inches thick (about 2 pounds total)
- 1 8-ounce package corn bread stuffing mix
- ⅓ cup dried currants or chopped raisins
- ¼ cup chopped hazelnuts or pecans, toasted (see tip, page 69)
- ¼ cup butter or margarine, melted
- 1 green onion, thinly sliced (about 2 tablespoons)
- 1 cup water
- 1 teaspoon instant chicken bouillon granules
- ⅓ cup currant, crab apple, or cherry jelly
- 1 tablespoon lemon juice or white wine vinegar
- ½ teaspoon ground ginger

Trim fat from chops. Cut a pocket in each chop by cutting a horizontal slit from the fat side almost to the bone. Set aside.

For stuffing, in a large bowl stir together stuffing mix, currants, nuts, melted butter, and onion. In another bowl stir together water and bouillon granules.

Toss *½ cup* of the stuffing mixture with *1 tablespoon* of the water mixture. Spoon into the pork chop pockets. If necessary, fasten openings of pockets with wooden toothpicks. Toss the remaining stuffing mixture with the remaining water mixture. Spoon into a greased 1-quart casserole; cover and refrigerate.

Place stuffed chops on convection roasting rack set on top of broiler pan. For glaze, in a small saucepan combine jelly, lemon juice, and ginger. Cook and stir until jelly melts. Brush tops of chops with some of the glaze.

Convection Bake pork chops in a **350°F** oven for 15 minutes. (Or, standard bake pork chops in a 375°F oven for 25 minutes.) Brush chops with the remaining glaze and return to oven. Place covered casserole with stuffing in the oven.

Convection Bake for 20 to 25 minutes or until pork is slightly pink in center and juices run clear, and stuffing is heated through. (Or, standard bake for 20 to 25 minutes.)
Makes 4 servings.

Honey-Glazed Pork Ribs

When you're in the mood for ribs, turn to this easy-to-fix version. It's extra moist and perfectly roasted in your convection oven.

- ⅔ cup catsup
- ¼ cup honey
- 1 teaspoon ground coriander or curry powder
- ¼ teaspoon garlic powder
- 2 to 3 pounds pork loin back ribs, cut into 2-rib portions

For glaze, in a small bowl stir together catsup, honey, coriander, and garlic powder. Set aside.

Place pork ribs, bone side down, in a shallow roasting pan.

Convection Roast in a **350°F** oven for 1 to 1¼ hours or until tender. (Or, standard roast in a 350°F oven for 1¼ to 1½ hours.) Drain fat. Brush ribs with some of the glaze.

Convection Roast for 15 minutes more, brushing once with the remaining glaze. (Or, standard roast for 15 minutes more, brushing once with the remaining glaze.)
Makes 4 servings.

Herb-Crusted Roast Pork

The roast makes a handsome centerpiece for your table. Trim it with fresh herbs or parsley sprigs and whole cranberries. To substitute dried herbs for fresh in the recipe, use one third the amount. (Pictured on the cover.)

- ½   cup fine dry bread crumbs
- 2   tablespoons snipped fresh sage
- 2   tablespoons snipped fresh thyme
- 1   tablespoon snipped fresh oregano
- 1   tablespoon snipped fresh basil
- ½   teaspoon pepper
- ¼   teaspoon salt
- 2   tablespoons butter or margarine, melted
- 1   3- to 4-pound pork loin center rib roast, backbone removed
- 2   tablespoons honey
- 1   16-ounce can whole cranberry sauce
- ¼   cup lemon juice

For topping, in a small bowl combine bread crumbs, sage, thyme, oregano, basil, pepper, and salt. Stir in melted butter. Set aside.

Trim fat from meat. With a sharp knife, score top of meat into a shallow diamond pattern. Place meat, rib side down, on convection roasting rack set on top of broiler pan. Insert meat probe or a meat thermometer into the center of the meat without touching bone.

Convection Roast in a **325°F** oven for 1¼ to 1¾ hours or until probe registers 155°F, brushing meat with honey and using a spatula to pat the topping over meat after 1 hour. (Or, standard roast in a 325°F oven for 1½ to 2 hours or until meat probe registers 155°F, brushing meat with honey and using a spatula to pat the topping over meat after 1 hour.)

Remove meat from pan, reserving the drippings. Cover meat with foil and let stand for 15 minutes before carving. (Temperature will rise during standing time.)

Meanwhile, for sauce, in a medium saucepan combine *2 tablespoons* of the drippings, the cranberry sauce, and lemon juice. Cook and stir until heated through.

To serve, slice meat between ribs. Serve cranberry sauce with meat.
Makes 8 to 10 servings.

Mustard Pork Roast

Dijon-style mustard gives this juicy roast a lovely golden color and a zestful flavor.

- 1   small onion, finely chopped (about ¼ cup)
- 2   tablespoons chicken broth or water
- 2   tablespoons Dijon-style mustard
- ¼   teaspoon dried marjoram, crushed
- ¼   teaspoon dried rosemary, crushed
- ⅛   teaspoon pepper
- 1   3- to 4-pound boneless pork top loin roast (double loin, tied)

In a small saucepan cook onion in chicken broth until tender. Stir in mustard, marjoram, rosemary, and pepper; set aside.

Trim fat from meat. Place meat on convection roasting rack set on top of broiler pan. Insert meat probe or a meat thermometer into the center of the meat.

Convection Roast in a **325°F** oven for 1½ to 2¼ hours or until probe registers 155°F, topping meat with the onion mixture after 1 hour. (Or, standard roast in a 325°F oven for 1¾ to 2½ hours, topping meat with the onion mixture after 1¼ hours.) Cover meat with foil and let stand for 10 minutes before carving. (Temperature will rise during standing time.)
Makes 12 to 14 servings.

Broiling Meats, Poultry, and Fish

Preheat on **Convection Broil** at **450°** for 5 minutes. (Or, preheat standard broiler.) Place meat, poultry, or fish on the grid of the unheated broiler pan. Place pan on rack position 4 or check the Use and Care Guide for suggested rack positions. **Convection Broil** with the oven door closed for the time given below, turning meat over after half of the broiling time. (Or, standard broil meat cuts less than 1¼ inches thick 3 to 4 inches from the heat; meat cuts 1¼ inches thick or thicker, all poultry, and all fish 4 to 5 inches from the heat. Broil with the door closed for the time given, turning meat over after half of the broiling time.)

Beef

Beef top loin, T-bone, sirloin, rib, or rib eye steaks
   (1 to 1¼ inches thick)

Convection	10 to 13 minutes (medium-rare)
	12 to 15 minutes (medium)
	17 to 20 minutes (well-done)
Standard	12 to 14 minutes (medium-rare)
	14 to 16 minutes (medium)
	18 to 22 minutes (well-done)

Beef tenderloin steaks (1 inch thick)

Convection	10 to 12 minutes (medium-rare)
	12 to 14 minutes (medium)
Standard	12 to 14 minutes (medium-rare)
	14 to 16 minutes (medium)

Pork

Pork loin, rib, or sirloin chops (1 inch thick)

Convection	16 to 18 minutes (medium)
Standard	16 to 18 minutes (medium)

Lamb

Lamb loin, rib, or sirloin chops (1 inch thick)

Convection	10 to 12 minutes (medium-rare)
	11 to 13 minutes (medium)
Standard	10 to 12 minutes (medium-rare)
	11 to 13 minutes (medium)

Ground meats

Ground beef, pork, or lamb patties (¾ inch thick)

Convection	15 to 17 minutes (well-done)
Standard	16 to 18 minutes (well-done)

Chicken

Chicken breast halves, skinless, boneless
   (4 ounces each)

Convection	7 to 10 minutes
Standard	12 to 15 minutes

Chicken breast halves, thighs, and/or drumsticks
   with bones (2 to 2½ pounds)

Convection	18 to 20 minutes
Standard	25 to 35 minutes

Fish

Fish fillets or steaks, fresh or thawed
   (½ to ¾ inch thick)

Convection	6 to 9 minutes
Standard	6 to 9 minutes

Spicy Red Snapper

Spicy Red Snapper

The exquisite flavor of the mango salsa depends on using fully ripe fruit. Choose a mango with a green or yellow skin tinged with red. The fruit should smell fragrant and feel fairly firm.

- 1   mango, peeled, seeded, and chopped (about 1½ cups)
- 1   medium red sweet pepper, finely chopped
- 2   green onions, thinly sliced (about ¼ cup)
- 1   fresh jalapeño pepper, seeded and finely chopped
- 3   tablespoons olive oil
- ½   teaspoon finely shredded lime peel
- 3   tablespoons lime juice, divided
- 1   tablespoon vinegar
- ½   teaspoon salt, divided
- ½   teaspoon pepper, divided
- 1   pound fresh or frozen red snapper fillets, ½ to ¾ inch thick
- 1   tablespoon water
- ½   teaspoon paprika
- ¼   teaspoon ground ginger
- ¼   teaspoon ground allspice
-    Lime wedges (optional)
-    Fresh cilantro sprigs or parsley sprigs (optional)

For salsa, in a medium bowl combine mango, red sweet pepper, onions, and jalapeño pepper. Add oil, lime peel, *2 tablespoons* of the lime juice, the vinegar, *¼ teaspoon* of the salt, and *¼ teaspoon* of the pepper.

Thaw fish, if frozen. Cut fish into 4 serving-size pieces. Combine the remaining 1 tablespoon lime juice and the water; brush mixture over fish. In a small bowl combine the remaining ¼ teaspoon salt, remaining ¼ teaspoon pepper, the paprika, ginger, and allspice. Rub onto fish. Place fish in a shallow baking pan, tucking under any thin edges so fish is a uniform thickness.

Convection Bake in a preheated **425°F** oven until fish just begins to flake easily with a fork. Allow 4 to 6 minutes per ½-inch thickness. (Or, standard bake in a preheated 450°F oven. Allow 4 to 6 minutes per ½-inch thickness.)

To serve, transfer fish to dinner plates. Brush fish with pan juices. Serve with salsa. If desired, garnish with lime and cilantro. *Makes 4 servings.*

Crunchy Broiled Fish

For a "fish-fry" supper, serve these crispy fillets with creamy coleslaw, buttered green beans, and corn bread.

- 1   pound fresh or frozen orange roughy, cod, or haddock fillets, ½ to ¾ inch thick
- 3   tablespoons all-purpose flour
- 3   tablespoons seasoned fine, dry bread crumbs
- 3   tablespoons cornmeal
- ¼   teaspoon lemon-pepper seasoning
-    Dash salt
- 3   tablespoons butter or margarine, melted

Thaw fish, if frozen. Cut fish into 4 serving-size pieces.

In a shallow dish combine flour, bread crumbs, cornmeal, lemon-pepper seasoning, and salt. Place melted butter in another shallow dish. Dip fish into melted butter, then dip into crumb mixture.

Preheat on **Convection Broil** at **450°F** for 5 minutes. (Or, preheat standard broiler.) Place fish on convection roasting rack set on top of broiler pan.

Convection Broil for 6 to 9 minutes or until fish just begins to flake easily with a fork, turning once. (Or, place directly on unheated broiler pan. Standard broil 4 to 5 inches from the heat for 6 to 9 minutes, turning once.) *Makes 4 servings.*

Walleye with Corn Salsa

Cilantro and jalapeño pepper give this Southwestern-style fish dish lots of pizzazz.

- 1 pound fresh or frozen walleye or lake trout fillets, ½ to ¾ inch thick
  Salt
  Pepper
- 1 cup frozen whole kernel corn
- ¼ cup water
- ½ cup small cherry tomatoes, quartered
- ½ cup finely chopped, peeled jicama
- ¼ cup snipped fresh cilantro or parsley
- 2 tablespoons lime juice
- 1 small fresh jalapeño pepper, seeded and finely chopped
  Dash salt
- 1 tablespoon Italian salad dressing
- ¼ teaspoon chili powder

Thaw fish, if frozen. Cut fish into 4 serving-size pieces. Sprinkle fish lightly with salt and pepper.

For salsa, in a small saucepan combine corn and water; bring to boiling. Reduce heat, cover, and simmer 5 minutes; drain.

In a medium bowl combine corn, tomatoes, jicama, cilantro, lime juice, jalapeño pepper, and salt. Set aside.

In a small bowl stir together Italian salad dressing and chili powder; brush over fish. Place fish in a greased 2-quart rectangular baking dish, tucking under any thin edges so fish is a uniform thickness.

Convection Bake in a preheated **425°F** oven until fish just begins to flake easily with a fork. Allow 4 to 6 minutes per ½-inch thickness. (Or, standard bake in a preheated 450°F oven. Allow 4 to 6 minutes per ½-inch thickness.) Serve fish with corn salsa.
Makes 4 servings.

Curried Crab Cakes with Chutney Tartar Sauce

Dress up any baked or broiled fish with this easy-to-fix sauce.

- 1 pound fresh or frozen lump crabmeat
- ½ cup fine dry bread crumbs
- 2 green onions, finely chopped (about ¼ cup)
- ½ teaspoon finely shredded orange peel
- ¼ cup orange juice
- 1 egg, beaten
- 2 tablespoons finely chopped celery
- 1 teaspoon curry powder
- ¼ cup plain yogurt
- 2 tablespoons mayonnaise or salad dressing
- 2 tablespoons chopped chutney
- 1 teaspoon balsamic vinegar or wine vinegar

Thaw crabmeat, if frozen. Drain well. Flake fresh or thawed crabmeat. In a large bowl combine crabmeat, bread crumbs, onions, orange peel, orange juice, egg, celery, and curry powder. Mix well. Using your hands, gently shape crab mixture into six ¾-inch-thick cakes. Place crab cakes in a greased shallow baking pan.

Convection Bake in a preheated **350°F** oven for 12 to 15 minutes or until crab cakes are lightly browned. (Or, standard bake in a preheated 350°F oven about 20 minutes.)

Meanwhile, for sauce, in a small bowl stir together yogurt, mayonnaise, chutney, and vinegar. Serve crab cakes with sauce.
Makes 6 servings.

Lake Trout Stuffed with Barley Pilaf

The orange sauce and fruited pilaf are also excellent with baked fish fillets or chicken.

- 1 2- to 2½-pound fresh or frozen whole, dressed lake trout or red snapper
- ⅔ cup quick-cooking barley
- ¾ teaspoon finely shredded orange peel, divided
- 2 oranges
- ¾ cup seedless red or green grapes, halved
- 1 stalk celery, sliced (about ½ cup)
- ½ teaspoon salt
- ¼ teaspoon dried thyme, crushed
   Salt and pepper
- 2 teaspoons cooking oil
- ⅔ cup orange juice
- ¼ cup water
- 2 teaspoons cornstarch
- 1 teaspoon soy sauce

Thaw fish, if frozen. Rinse fish; pat dry with paper towels.

For pilaf, cook barley according to package directions. Meanwhile, peel and section oranges over a medium bowl to catch the juice. Chop orange sections and add to the reserved juice in bowl. Stir in cooked barley, *¼ teaspoon* of the orange peel, the grapes, celery, the ½ teaspoon salt, and thyme.

Place fish in a well-greased shallow baking pan. Sprinkle the cavity lightly with salt and pepper. Spoon about *1 cup* of the pilaf into the cavity; press lightly to flatten. Brush fish with cooking oil. Spoon the remaining pilaf into a 1-quart casserole; cover casserole.

Convection Bake fish and the covered casserole with pilaf in a preheated **325°F** oven for 35 to 40 minutes or until fish just begins to flake easily with a fork and pilaf is heated through. (Or, standard bake in a preheated 350°F oven for 30 to 40 minutes.)

Meanwhile, for sauce, in a small saucepan stir together the remaining ½ teaspoon orange peel, the ⅔ cup orange juice, water, cornstarch, and soy sauce. Cook and stir over medium heat until thickened and bubbly. Cook and stir for 2 minutes more.

To serve, transfer stuffed fish to a serving platter. Spoon stuffing from casserole onto platter. Pass the sauce to spoon over fish. *Makes 4 servings.*

Convenient Convection Oven Meals

Fix-and-forget oven meals free you from the kitchen so you can spend more time with your guests or family. When planning an oven meal, keep these tips in mind:

- Select recipes that cook at similar temperatures.
- Make sure all the baking pans for items in the menu will fit in your oven at one time. Allow at least 1 inch of space around the edges of the pans.
- For good air circulation, stagger the pans at different levels and be sure the pans don't touch the sides of the oven.
- If the oven will be quite full, allow a few extra minutes of cooking time.
- To keep heat loss to a minimum, open the oven only when necessary.

Garden Zucchini Pie

Garden Zucchini Pie

4   eggs
1   small onion, finely chopped (about ¼ cup)
¼   cup grated Parmesan cheese
3   cups shredded potatoes (about 6 medium potatoes)
2   medium zucchini, thinly sliced (about 2½ cups)
1   clove garlic, minced
1   tablespoon butter or margarine
¾   cup shredded cheddar or Swiss cheese (3 ounces)
½   cup milk
½   teaspoon dried oregano, crushed
¼   teaspoon salt
¼   teaspoon pepper
     Small fresh oregano leaves (optional)

In a large bowl combine *1* of the eggs, the onion, and Parmesan cheese. Stir in potatoes. Transfer mixture to a 10-inch quiche dish or a 9-inch pie plate. Pat onto the bottom and up the sides of the dish.

Convection Bake in a preheated **400°F** oven for 15 to 20 minutes or until golden brown. (Or, standard bake in a preheated 400°F oven for 35 to 40 minutes.) Remove; set on a wire rack. Reduce **Convection Bake** temperature to **325°F.** (Reduce standard oven temperature to 350°F.)

In a large skillet cook zucchini and garlic in butter until zucchini is tender-crisp; cool slightly. Arrange on top of potato crust. In a small bowl beat together the remaining 3 eggs, shredded cheese, milk, dried oregano, salt, and pepper. Set the quiche dish or pie plate on oven rack. Carefully pour egg mixture over zucchini mixture in pie plate.

Convection Bake for 25 to 30 minutes or until a knife inserted near the center comes out clean. (Or, standard bake for 25 to 30 minutes.) Let stand for 10 minutes before serving. If desired, sprinkle with fresh oregano leaves.
Makes 6 servings.

Broccoli-Chèvre Soufflé

When preparing this novel soufflé, you can substitute cream cheese or crumbled feta cheese for the chèvre, if you prefer.

1   small onion, chopped (about ¼ cup)
1   clove garlic, minced
3   tablespoons olive oil or cooking oil
¼   cup all-purpose flour
2   tablespoons snipped fresh basil or 1 teaspoon dried basil, crushed
¼   teaspoon pepper
1   cup milk
1   cup crumbled chèvre cheese (goat cheese) (4 ounces)
1   cup finely chopped cooked broccoli
3   eggs

In a medium saucepan cook onion and garlic in oil until onion is tender but not brown. Stir in flour, basil, and pepper. Add milk all at once. Cook and stir over medium heat until thickened and bubbly. Remove from heat. Stir in chèvre cheese until melted. Stir in broccoli.

Separate eggs, reserving the egg whites. In a medium mixing bowl beat egg yolks slightly with a fork. Gradually add broccoli mixture, stirring constantly.

In another medium bowl beat egg whites with an electric mixer on high speed until stiff peaks form (tips stand straight). Gently fold about 1 cup of the beaten egg whites into the broccoli mixture. Gradually pour the broccoli mixture over the remaining egg whites, folding to combine. Pour into a 1½-quart soufflé dish.

Convection Bake in a preheated **325°F** oven for 35 to 40 minutes or until a knife inserted near the center comes out clean. (Or, standard bake in a preheated 350°F oven about 40 minutes.) Serve immediately.
Makes 4 servings.

Spinach Soufflé Quiche

For a light supper, serve this delicate cheese pie with a crisp tossed salad or colorful fruit salad.

Pastry for Single-Crust Pie (see recipe, page 81)
4 slices bacon, chopped
1 medium onion, chopped (about ½ cup)
3 cups lightly packed chopped fresh spinach
2 tablespoons water
8 eggs
½ cup dairy sour cream
1 tablespoon all-purpose flour
½ cup light cream, half and half, or milk
¼ teaspoon salt
⅛ teaspoon white pepper
Dash ground nutmeg (optional)
⅔ cup shredded mozzarella cheese (2½ ounces)
½ cup shredded Swiss cheese (2 ounces)
Plum tomato slices (optional)

Prepare Pastry for Single-Crust Pie. On a lightly floured surface, roll dough into a 12-inch circle. Fit into a 9-inch pie plate, being careful not to stretch pastry. Trim to ½ inch beyond edge of pie plate; fold under extra pastry. Make a high fluted edge.

Line pastry shell with a double thickness of foil, then add enough dry beans to cover plate bottom and hold down foil.

Convection Roast in a preheated **425°F** oven for 8 minutes. (Or, standard bake in a preheated 450°F oven for 8 minutes.) Remove beans and foil. (*Do not* reuse beans in cooking.)

Convection Roast for 4 to 5 minutes more or until pastry is golden brown. (Or, standard bake for 4 to 5 minutes more.) Remove from oven; cool on a wire rack.

Reduce **Convection Roast** temperature to **300°F.** (Reduce standard oven temperature to 300°F.)

Meanwhile, in a skillet cook bacon until crisp. Drain on paper towels. Reserve *1 tablespoon* of the drippings in skillet.

Cook onion in the reserved drippings over medium heat until tender. Stir in spinach and water. Cover and cook for 3 minutes. Drain well.

In a medium bowl beat eggs slightly with a fork. Combine sour cream and flour; add to eggs. Stir in cream, salt, pepper, and, if desired, nutmeg. Stir in mozzarella cheese, Swiss cheese, bacon, and spinach mixture. Set the pastry shell on oven rack. Carefully pour spinach mixture into pastry shell.

Convection Roast about 40 minutes or until a knife inserted near the center comes out clean. (Or, standard bake for 45 to 50 minutes. If necessary, cover edge of crust with foil the last 15 to 20 minutes to prevent overbrowning.)

Let stand for 10 minutes before serving. If desired, garnish with tomato slices.
Makes 6 to 8 servings.

Lamb Chops Teriyaki

Brush on lots of this flavor-packed sauce to give the chops an extraordinary Oriental zing.

- 4 lamb sirloin chops or 8 lamb rib chops, cut 1 inch thick (about 1½ pounds total)
- 2 tablespoons brown sugar
- 2 tablespoons soy sauce
- 1 tablespoon catsup
- 1½ teaspoons lemon juice
- 1 teaspoon grated fresh gingerroot or ¼ teaspoon ground ginger
- ⅛ teaspoon garlic powder
- ⅛ teaspoon pepper

Trim fat from chops. For sauce, in a small bowl stir together brown sugar, soy sauce, catsup, lemon juice, ginger, garlic powder, and pepper. Set aside.

Meanwhile, preheat on **Convection Broil** at **450°F** for 5 minutes. (Or, preheat standard broiler.) Place lamb chops on the unheated broiler pan.

Convection Broil to desired doneness, turning once and brushing with sauce the last 2 to 3 minutes of cooking. Allow 10 to 12 minutes for medium-rare or 11 to 13 minutes for medium. (Or, standard broil 3 to 4 inches from the heat, turning once and brushing with sauce the last 2 to 3 minutes of cooking. Allow 10 to 12 minutes for medium-rare or 11 to 13 minutes for medium.)
Makes 4 servings.

East Indian Leg of Lamb

When handling the jalapeños, slip plastic bags over your hands or wear plastic gloves to prevent the oils in the peppers from burning your skin.

- 1 4- to 5-pound leg of lamb
- 1 large onion, cut up (about 1 cup)
- 4 fresh or canned jalapeño peppers, seeded and cut up
- 3 cloves garlic, halved
- 3 tablespoons lime juice
- 1 tablespoon honey
- 1 teaspoon salt
- 1 teaspoon Dijon-style mustard
- ½ teaspoon pepper
- ¼ teaspoon ground ginger
- 2 tablespoons butter or margarine, melted

Remove fell (paper-thin, pinkish-red layer) from surface of meat. Trim fat from meat. In a blender container or food processor bowl combine onion, jalapeños, garlic, lime juice, honey, salt, mustard, pepper, and ginger. Cover and blend or process until nearly smooth, stopping and scraping sides as necessary. Set aside.

For easier cleanup, line the bottom of broiler pan with heavy foil. Place meat, trimmed side up, on convection roasting rack set on top of broiler pan. Insert meat probe or a meat thermometer into the thickest portion of the meat without touching bone.

Convection Roast in a **325°F** oven for 1¼ to 1½ hours for medium-rare or until probe registers 140°F, spooning honey mixture over meat and drizzling with melted butter after 45 minutes. (Or, standard roast in a 325°F oven for 1¼ to 1¾ hours, spooning honey mixture over meat and drizzling with butter after 45 minutes.)

Cover meat with foil and let stand for 15 minutes before carving. (Temperature will rise during standing time.)
Makes 12 to 16 servings.

Fennel-Lemon Roasted Vegetables (see recipe, page 48)

Savory Vegetable Dishes

For a change of pace, make the vegetable the star of the meal. Create intriguing new meals by teaming the flavorsome convection-cooked vegetables in this chapter with simple main dishes. Try Fennel-Lemon Roasted Vegetables with fish, Cheesy Cauliflower Bake with beef, or Maple Sweet Potato Casserole with chicken. The possibilities are endless.

Fennel-Lemon Roasted Vegetables

This rainbow of vegetables will be the highlight of any meal. (Pictured on pages 46–47.)

- 8   ounces tiny new potatoes, halved, or 2 small potatoes, cut into eighths
- 2   small red, green, or yellow sweet peppers, cut up
- 1   fennel bulb or 3 stalks celery,* sliced ½ inch thick (about 1½ cups)
- 1   medium chayote, zucchini, or yellow summer squash, cut into 1-inch cubes
- 1   small red onion, cut into wedges
- 3   cloves garlic, peeled and chopped
- ½   teaspoon finely shredded lemon peel
- 2   tablespoons lemon juice
- 2   tablespoons olive oil or cooking oil
- ½   teaspoon granulated sugar
- ¼   teaspoon salt
- ⅛   teaspoon pepper
- 3   tablespoons sliced, pitted ripe olives

In a greased 13x9x2-inch baking pan combine potatoes, sweet peppers, fennel, squash, onion, and garlic.

In a small bowl combine lemon peel, lemon juice, oil, sugar, salt, and pepper. Drizzle over vegetables, tossing to coat vegetables evenly.

Convection Roast in a **425°F** oven for 25 to 30 minutes or until vegetables are tender, stirring twice. (Or, standard bake in a 450°F oven about 40 minutes, stirring twice.) Transfer to a serving bowl. Sprinkle with olives.
Makes 4 servings.

*Note: If using celery, stir ¼ teaspoon crushed *fennel seed* into the lemon mixture.

Crispy Potato Wedges

Hot and crisp from the oven, these cheese-coated potatoes are a fabulous alternative to french fries.

- 2   medium baking potatoes
- 1   medium sweet potato or yam
- 2   tablespoons cooking oil
- 1   tablespoon grated Parmesan cheese
- 1   teaspoon paprika
- ½   teaspoon garlic salt
- ½   teaspoon dried thyme, crushed
- ¼   teaspoon pepper

Scrub potatoes; pat dry. Cut each potato lengthwise into 8 wedges. Arrange wedges, cut side up, in a 15x10x1-inch baking pan.

In a small bowl combine oil, Parmesan cheese, paprika, garlic salt, thyme, and pepper. Brush the Parmesan mixture onto potato wedges.

Convection Bake in a preheated **375°F** oven for 25 to 30 minutes or until potatoes are tender and potato skins are crisp. (Or, standard bake in a preheated 375°F oven for 45 to 55 minutes.)
Makes 4 to 6 servings.

Vegetable Pasta Casserole

The combination of varied flavors makes this colorful casserole one you'll prepare again and again. If you don't have bow-tie pasta on hand, make it with corkscrew or rotini pasta.

3	cups green beans bias-sliced into 2-inch pieces
2½	cups medium bow-tie pasta (about 6 ounces)
2	medium yellow summer squash, cut into thin strips (about 3 cups)
5	ounces fresh mushrooms, sliced (about 2 cups)
1	large onion, chopped (about 1 cup)
3	tablespoons snipped fresh basil or 1½ teaspoons dried basil, crushed
2	tablespoons snipped fresh oregano or 1 teaspoon dried oregano, crushed
2	tablespoons butter or margarine
3	tablespoons all-purpose flour
½	teaspoon salt
¼	teaspoon pepper
3	cups milk
¾	cup shredded process Swiss cheese (3 ounces)
1	to 2 tablespoons Dijon-style mustard Few drops bottled hot pepper sauce
4	to 6 plum tomatoes, diagonally sliced (about 2 cups)
1	cup soft bread crumbs (about 1½ slices)
¼	cup grated Parmesan cheese

In a large saucepan or Dutch oven cook green beans, loosely covered, in a large amount of boiling, lightly salted water for 5 minutes. Add bow-tie pasta. Return to boiling; boil gently, uncovered, for 5 minutes more. Add squash. Return to boiling; boil gently about 5 minutes more or until pasta is tender. Drain mixture. Return to saucepan.

Meanwhile, in a large skillet cook mushrooms, onion, basil, and oregano in butter until vegetables are tender. Stir in flour, salt, and pepper. Add milk all at once. Cook and stir over medium heat until slightly thickened and bubbly. Stir in Swiss cheese, mustard, and hot pepper sauce. Cook and stir over low heat about 1 minute more or until cheese is melted.

Pour the cheese mixture over pasta mixture; toss gently to combine. Add the tomatoes; toss gently. Transfer mixture to a 3-quart rectangular baking dish.

For topping, stir together bread crumbs and Parmesan cheese. Sprinkle the topping over casserole.

Convection Bake in a preheated **375°F** oven for 20 to 25 minutes or until mixture is heated through. (Or, standard bake in a preheated 400°F oven for 20 to 25 minutes.) *Makes 10 to 12 servings.*

To make ahead: Assemble the casserole and prepare the topping as directed above, *except* cover and refrigerate separately for up to 24 hours. To serve, sprinkle topping over chilled casserole. **Convection Bake** in a preheated 375°F oven about 30 minutes or until heated through. (Or, standard bake in a preheated 400°F oven about 35 minutes.)

Baked Stuffed Tomatoes

Baked Stuffed Tomatoes

This versatile vegetable goes well with a roast or chicken. Put the tomatoes into the oven with the meat for the last 15 minutes of cooking.

    4   firm medium tomatoes
    2   cloves garlic, minced
    1   tablespoon butter or margarine
    1   small green pepper, chopped (about ½ cup)
    1   tablespoon snipped fresh basil or 1 teaspoon
          dried basil, crushed
    ¾   cup plain or seasoned croutons
    2   tablespoons snipped parsley

Cut a ½-inch slice from the top of each tomato; discard tops. Scoop out the pulp; discard seeds. Coarsely chop the tomato pulp (you should have about 1 cup). Set aside.

In a medium skillet cook garlic in butter over medium heat for 30 seconds. Stir in tomato pulp, green pepper, and basil. Cook about 2 minutes more or until green pepper is tender-crisp. Stir in croutons and parsley.

Spoon the crouton mixture into hollowed-out tomatoes. Arrange the stuffed tomatoes in a 9-inch pie plate.

Convection Bake in a preheated **325°F** oven about 15 minutes or until heated through. (Or, standard bake in a preheated 350°F oven about 15 minutes.)
Makes 4 servings.

Eggplant with Two-Cheese Sauce

These delectable eggplant slices are a grand way to introduce new vegetables to your family.

    1   medium eggplant (about 1 pound)
    3   tablespoons butter or margarine, divided
    1   medium green or red sweet pepper, chopped
          (about ¾ cup)
    2   tablespoons snipped fresh basil or 1 teaspoon
          dried basil, crushed
    1   clove garlic, minced
    2   tablespoons all-purpose flour
    1   cup milk
    ¼   cup grated Parmesan cheese
    1   tablespoon dry white wine (optional)
    ½   cup shredded cheddar cheese (2 ounces)
    2   tablespoons snipped parsley

Peel eggplant; cut crosswise into ½-inch-thick slices.

In a large skillet cook *half* of the eggplant at a time in *2 tablespoons* of the butter for 4 to 6 minutes or until lightly browned, turning once. (If necessary, add more butter.) Place eggplant slices in a 2-quart square baking dish.

In the same skillet cook green pepper, basil, and garlic in the remaining 1 tablespoon butter until pepper is tender. Stir in flour. Add milk all at once. Cook and stir over medium heat until thickened and bubbly. Stir in Parmesan cheese and, if desired, white wine. Pour the Parmesan mixture over eggplant slices in dish. Sprinkle with cheddar cheese.

Convection Bake in a preheated **325°F** oven for 8 to 10 minutes or until heated through and cheddar cheese melts. (Or, standard bake in a preheated 350°F oven about 15 minutes.) Sprinkle with parsley.
Makes 4 to 6 servings.

Cheesy Cauliflower Bake

A creamy Swiss cheese sauce with a hint of nutmeg is the ideal way to dress up vegetables.

- 4 slices bacon, chopped
- 1 medium onion, chopped (about ½ cup)
- 2 cloves garlic, minced
- 1 medium cauliflower, cut into flowerets (about 5 cups)
- 2 medium carrots, thinly sliced (about 1 cup)
- ⅓ cup water
- 1 cup milk
- 2 tablespoons all-purpose flour
- ¼ teaspoon pepper
- ⅛ teaspoon salt
- ⅛ teaspoon ground nutmeg
- ¾ cup shredded Swiss cheese (3 ounces), divided
- ¾ cup soft bread crumbs (about 1 slice)
- 2 tablespoons butter or margarine, melted

In a large saucepan cook bacon until crisp. Drain bacon on paper towels. Reserve *2 tablespoons* of the drippings in saucepan. Cook onion and garlic in the reserved drippings over medium heat for 2 minutes. Add cauliflower, carrots, and water. Cover and simmer for 5 to 7 minutes or until vegetables are just tender-crisp.

In a screw-top jar combine milk, flour, pepper, salt, and nutmeg. Cover and shake until well mixed. Add to vegetables. Cook and stir over medium heat until thickened and bubbly. Add bacon and *½ cup* of the Swiss cheese, stirring until cheese melts.

Transfer to a 1½-quart casserole. Combine crumbs, melted butter, and the remaining ¼ cup Swiss cheese. Sprinkle over casserole.

Convection Bake in a preheated **375°F** oven about 10 minutes or until crumbs are golden brown. (Or, standard bake in a preheated 375°F oven for 12 to 15 minutes.)
Makes 6 servings.

Maple Sweet Potato Casserole

Looking for a new way to serve potatoes? Try them mashed in this maple-flavored dish.

- 4 medium sweet potatoes or yams (about 1⅓ pounds total) or one 18-ounce can sweet potatoes, drained
- 1 egg
- ½ cup evaporated milk
- 2 tablespoons butter or margarine
- ½ cup chopped, pitted whole dates
- 2 tablespoons maple syrup or maple-flavored syrup
- 1 tablespoon butter or margarine, melted

Peel fresh sweet potatoes; cut potatoes into quarters or cubes. In a large saucepan combine sweet potatoes and enough salted water to cover; bring to boiling. Reduce heat, cover, and simmer for 25 to 35 minutes or until tender. Drain.

Place sweet potatoes in a large mixing bowl. Add egg and evaporated milk. Beat with an electric mixer on medium-low speed until smooth.

In the same large saucepan melt the 2 tablespoons butter. Add dates. Cook and stir 2 minutes. Stir mixture into sweet potato mixture. Transfer to a 1-quart casserole.

For topping, combine maple syrup and the 1 tablespoon melted butter. Pour over sweet potato mixture.

Convection Bake in a preheated **350°F** oven for 18 to 20 minutes or until heated through. (Or, standard bake in a preheated 350°F oven for 25 to 30 minutes.)
Makes 4 servings.

Carrot and Rice Casserole

This cheese-flavored dish is also good made with shredded sweet potatoes.

6	to 8 medium carrots, shredded (about 3 cups)
1	cup water
¼	cup long grain rice
2	green onions, sliced (about ¼ cup)
¼	teaspoon salt
⅛	teaspoon pepper
1¼	cups shredded American or cheddar cheese (5 ounces), divided
¾	cup milk
1	egg, beaten

In a medium saucepan combine carrots, water, uncooked rice, green onions, salt, and pepper; bring to boiling. Reduce heat, cover, and simmer for 20 minutes. *Do not drain.* Stir in *1 cup* of the cheese, the milk, and egg. Transfer to a 9-inch pie plate.

Convection Roast in a preheated **325°F** oven for 15 to 20 minutes or until set. (Or, standard bake in a preheated 350°F oven about 20 minutes.)

Sprinkle casserole with remaining ¼ cup cheese. Let stand for 10 minutes before serving. Cut into wedges.

Makes 6 servings.

Saucy Broccoli-Onion Bake

Create an oven meal by cooking this creamy vegetable dish with roast beef or pork.

2	cups chopped fresh broccoli or one 10-ounce package frozen cut broccoli
1	medium onion, cut into thin wedges, or 1 cup frozen small whole onions
1	tablespoon butter or margarine
1	tablespoon all-purpose flour
½	teaspoon dried basil, oregano, or marjoram, crushed
¼	teaspoon salt
¼	teaspoon pepper
⅔	cup milk
3	ounces cream cheese, cut up
¾	cup soft bread crumbs (1 slice)
1	tablespoon butter or margarine, melted

In a medium saucepan cook broccoli and onions, covered, in a small amount of boiling water for 4 minutes. Drain well, removing vegetables from saucepan.

In the same saucepan melt 1 tablespoon butter. Stir in flour, herb, salt, and pepper. Add milk all at once. Cook and stir over medium heat until thickened and bubbly. Add cream cheese, stirring until melted. Stir in broccoli and onions. Transfer to a 1-quart casserole.

In a small bowl stir together bread crumbs and melted butter. Sprinkle crumbs over broccoli mixture.

Convection Roast in a preheated **325°F** oven for 15 to 20 minutes or until heated through. (Or, standard bake in a preheated 350°F oven for 15 to 20 minutes.)

Makes 4 servings.

Bountiful Breads

When only a crusty homemade loaf of bread, tender muffin, or flaky biscuit straight from the oven will do, turn to the recipes in this chapter. You'll find everything from simple Baguettes and glorious Caramel-Pecan Rolls to easy Parmesan Corn Bread Puffs. Convection Bake these breads and delight your family and friends with the outstanding results.

Sweet Potato-Wheat Twists (see recipe, page 56)

Sweet Potato-Wheat Twists

This rich-hued honey-flavored bread is delicious toasted and spread with preserves. (Pictured on pages 54–55.)

1¼   cups water
1   cup chopped peeled sweet potato (about 1 medium)
1   cup buttermilk or sour milk (see tip, page 71)
2   tablespoons butter or margarine
2   tablespoons honey
2   teaspoons salt
5   to 5½ cups all-purpose flour, divided
2   packages active dry yeast
1   egg
1½   cups whole wheat flour

In a medium saucepan combine water and sweet potato; bring to boiling. Reduce heat, cover, and simmer about 12 minutes or until very tender. *Do not drain.* Mash the potato in the water. Measure potato mixture and, if necessary, add water to equal 1½ cups.

Return potato mixture to the saucepan. Add buttermilk, butter, honey, and salt. Heat or cool, as necessary, and stir until warm (120°F to 130°F) and butter is almost melted.

In a large mixing bowl combine *2 cups* of the all-purpose flour and the yeast. Add potato mixture and egg. Beat with an electric mixer on low speed for 30 seconds, scraping sides of bowl constantly. Beat on high speed for 3 minutes. Divide the batter in half.

To *half* of the batter, stir in the whole wheat flour and ½ *cup* of the all-purpose flour. Turn out onto a lightly floured surface. Knead in enough of the remaining all-purpose flour (¼ to ½ cup) to make a moderately stiff dough that is smooth and elastic (6 to 8 minutes total). Shape into a ball. Place in a lightly greased bowl; turn once to grease surface. Cover and let rise in a warm place until double (about 45 minutes).

To the remaining batter, stir in *2 cups* of the all-purpose flour. Turn out onto a lightly floured surface. Knead in enough of the remaining all-purpose flour (¼ to ½ cup) to make a moderately stiff dough that is smooth and elastic (6 to 8 minutes total). Shape into a ball. Place in a lightly greased bowl; turn once. Cover and let rise until double (about 45 minutes).

Punch down each ball of dough. Turn out onto a lightly floured surface. Divide each in half. Cover and let rest for 10 minutes.

Roll each portion of dough into an evenly thick 10-inch-long rope. For each loaf, loosely twist 1 plain and 1 whole wheat rope together; press ends together to seal. Place in 2 lightly greased 9x5x3-inch loaf pans. Cover and let rise in a warm place until nearly double (30 to 40 minutes).

Convection Bake in a preheated **350°F** oven 30 to 35 minutes or until loaves sound hollow when tapped. (Or, standard bake in a preheated 375°F oven about 40 minutes. If necessary, cover loosely with foil the last 10 minutes to prevent overbrowning.) Remove from pans. Cool on racks.
Makes 2 loaves.

Pepper-Cheese Bread

Combine this zesty bread with roast beef for a terrific sandwich.

2¾ to 3¼ cups all-purpose flour, divided
1 package active dry yeast
1 to 1½ teaspoons cracked peppercorns
½ teaspoon salt
1 cup warm water (120°F to 130°F)
2 tablespoons olive oil or cooking oil
¾ cup shredded provolone cheese (3 ounces)
½ cup grated Parmesan or Romano cheese
1 egg white, slightly beaten
1 tablespoon water

In a large mixing bowl stir together *1 cup* of the flour, the yeast, peppercorns, and salt. Add the 1 cup warm water and the oil.

Beat with an electric mixer on low speed for 30 seconds, scraping sides of bowl constantly. Beat on high speed for 3 minutes. Using a spoon, stir in as much remaining flour as you can.

Turn out onto a lightly floured surface. Knead in enough of the remaining flour to make a stiff dough that is smooth and elastic (8 to 10 minutes total). Shape into a ball. Place in a lightly greased bowl; turn once to grease surface. Cover and let rise in a warm place until double (1 to 1¼ hours).

Punch dough down. Turn out onto a lightly floured surface. Divide in half. Cover and let rest for 10 minutes. Roll each half of the dough into a 12x8-inch rectangle. Sprinkle each rectangle with *half* of the provolone cheese and *half* of the Parmesan cheese. Roll up dough jelly-roll style, starting from a long side. Moisten edge with water and seal. Taper ends.

Place loaves, seam sides down, on a lightly greased large baking sheet.

In a small bowl stir together egg white and the 1 tablespoon water; brush some of the mixture over loaves. Cover and let rise in a warm place until nearly double (about 45 minutes).

Using a sharp knife, make 3 or 4 shallow diagonal cuts across top of each loaf.

Convection Bake in a preheated **350°F** oven for 25 to 30 minutes or until loaves sound hollow when tapped, brushing with egg white mixture after 15 minutes. (Or, standard bake in a preheated 375°F oven for 30 to 35 minutes, brushing with egg white mixture after 15 minutes.) Remove loaves from baking sheet. Cool on a wire rack. *Makes 2 loaves.*

■ Oven-Proofing Yeast Doughs ■

Your convection oven is the ideal place to proof yeast breads. To create optimum conditions in your oven, use this easy method.

Put the dough in a lightly greased bowl, loosely cover with waxed paper coated with shortening, and position the bowl of dough on a rack in your *unheated* convection oven. Place a baking dish filled with 2 cups of boiling water on the floor of the oven and close the oven door. Press and hold the Baked Goods pad for 5 seconds. Start the oven and let the dough rise for the time specified in your recipe or until the dough is nearly double in size.

To see if the dough has risen enough and is ready for shaping, press 2 fingers about ½ inch into the dough. If the indentation remains after you remove your fingers, the dough is ready to be punched down and shaped. When proofing is done, turn off the oven.

Cucumber Buns

Cucumber Buns

3¼ to 3¾ cups all-purpose flour, divided
1 package active dry yeast
2 tablespoons snipped fresh chives
¼ teaspoon dried dillweed
1 medium cucumber, peeled and cut up
½ cup dairy sour cream
¼ cup water
1 tablespoon granulated sugar
¾ teaspoon salt

In a large mixing bowl combine *1¼ cups* of the flour, the yeast, chives, and dillweed.

Place cucumber in a food processor bowl or blender container. Cover and process or blend until smooth. Measure ¾ cup puree; discard any remaining puree. In a medium saucepan heat and stir the cucumber puree, sour cream, water, sugar, and salt until warm (120°F to 130°F). (Mixture will look curdled.) Add to flour mixture. Beat with an electric mixer on low speed for 30 seconds, scraping sides of bowl constantly. Beat on high speed for 3 minutes. Using a spoon, stir in as much remaining flour as you can.

Turn out onto a lightly floured surface. Knead in enough of the remaining flour to make a moderately stiff dough that is smooth and elastic (6 to 8 minutes total). Shape into a ball. Place in a lightly greased bowl; turn once. Cover and let rise in a warm place until double (about 45 minutes).

Punch down. Turn out onto a lightly floured surface. Cover and let rest for 10 minutes. Divide into 12 pieces and shape into balls. Place in a greased 13x9x2-inch baking pan. Cover and let rise in a warm place until nearly double (about 30 minutes).

Convection Bake in a preheated **350°F** oven for 18 to 20 minutes or until lightly browned. (Or, standard bake in a preheated 350°F oven for 20 to 25 minutes.) Serve warm or cool.

Makes 12 rolls.

Festive Holiday Brioches

1 package active dry yeast
¼ cup warm water (105°F to 115°F)
½ cup butter or margarine, softened
⅓ cup granulated sugar
½ teaspoon salt
4 cups all-purpose flour, divided
⅔ cup milk
4 eggs
½ cup dried cranberries or dried cherries
1 tablespoon granulated sugar

Soften yeast in warm water. In a large mixing bowl beat butter, the ⅓ cup sugar, and salt until fluffy. Add *1 cup* of the flour and the milk. Separate *1* of the eggs. Add the yolk and the 3 whole eggs to flour mixture. (Cover and refrigerate remaining egg white.) Add the softened yeast to flour mixture; beat well. Chop cranberries; stir into flour mixture. Stir in the remaining flour.

Place in a greased bowl; turn once to grease surface. Cover and let rise in a warm place until double (about 2 hours), then refrigerate for 6 to 24 hours.

Stir dough. Turn out onto lightly floured surface. Divide into 4 portions. Set 1 portion aside. Divide each of the remaining portions into 8 pieces. Shape into balls. Place into well-greased 2½-inch muffin cups. Divide reserved portion into 24 pieces; shape into balls. Make an indentation in each large ball. Press a small ball into each indentation.

Combine the reserved egg white and the 1 tablespoon sugar. Brush over rolls. Cover and let rise in a warm place until nearly double (about 45 minutes).

Convection Bake in a preheated **350°F** oven for 12 to 14 minutes or until golden brown. (Or, standard bake in a preheated 375°F oven about 15 minutes.) Remove from pans. Cool slightly on wire racks. Serve warm or cool.

Makes 24 rolls.

Wild Rice Bread

The texture of the wild rice and the carrot flecks of color make this a deliciously different bread.

⅓	cup wild rice
1	cup water
4	to 4½ cups all-purpose flour, divided
2	packages active dry yeast
¾	cup milk
¼	cup butter or margarine
¼	cup honey
1	teaspoon salt
1	egg, beaten
2	carrots, finely shredded (about 1 cup)
1	egg yolk, beaten
1	tablespoon water

Rinse wild rice well. In a small saucepan bring wild rice and the 1 cup water to boiling. Reduce heat, cover, and simmer for 40 to 50 minutes or until wild rice is tender. Drain and cool.

In a large mixing bowl stir together *1½ cups* of the flour and the yeast. In a medium saucepan heat and stir milk, butter, honey, and salt until warm (120°F to 130°F) and butter is almost melted. Add to flour mixture; add egg. Beat with an electric mixer on low speed for 30 seconds, scraping sides of bowl constantly. Beat on high speed for 3 minutes. Using a spoon, stir in rice, carrots, and as much of the remaining flour as you can.

Turn out onto a lightly floured surface. Knead in enough of the remaining flour to make a moderately stiff dough that is smooth and elastic (6 to 8 minutes total). Shape into a ball. Place in a lightly greased bowl; turn once to grease surface.

Cover and let rise in a warm place until double (about 1 hour). Punch dough down. Turn out onto a lightly floured surface. Divide dough in half. Cover and let rest for 10 minutes. Shape each half of dough into a 9x3-inch loaf. Place on a lightly greased large baking sheet.

Cover and let rise in a warm place until nearly double (about 30 minutes). In a small bowl combine egg yolk and the 1 tablespoon water. Cover and refrigerate until needed. Using a sharp knife, make 3 or 4 shallow diagonal cuts across top of each loaf.

Convection Bake in a preheated **350°F** oven about 25 minutes or until loaves sound hollow when tapped, brushing with egg yolk mixture after 20 minutes. (Or, standard bake in a preheated 375°F oven about 25 minutes, brushing with egg yolk mixture after 20 minutes.) Remove loaves from baking sheet. Cool on wire racks.
Makes 2 loaves.

Baguettes

An appealing addition to any meal, these slim loaves are especially crusty on the outside and soft and chewy on the inside, thanks to convection baking.

5½	to 6 cups all-purpose flour, divided
2	packages active dry yeast
1½	teaspoons salt
2	cups warm water (120°F to 130°F)
	Yellow cornmeal
1	egg white, slightly beaten
1	tablespoon water

In a large mixing bowl combine *2 cups* of the flour, the yeast, and salt. Add the 2 cups warm water. Beat with an electric mixer on low speed for 30 seconds, scraping sides of bowl constantly. Beat on high speed for 3 minutes. Using a spoon, stir in as much of the remaining flour as you can.

Turn out onto a lightly floured surface. Knead in enough of the remaining flour to make a stiff dough that is smooth and elastic (8 to 10 minutes total). Shape into a ball. Place in a lightly greased bowl; turn once to grease surface. Cover and let rise in a warm place until double (about 1 hour).

Punch dough down. Turn out onto a lightly floured surface. Divide into quarters. Cover and let rest for 10 minutes. Roll each portion into a 12x8-inch rectangle. Roll up dough jelly-roll style, starting from a long side. Seal seam. Taper ends.

Place, seam sides down, on greased baking sheets sprinkled with cornmeal. Cover and let rise in a warm place until nearly double (35 to 45 minutes). With a sharp knife, make 3 or 4 shallow diagonal cuts across top of each loaf. In a small bowl combine egg white and the 1 tablespoon water. Brush egg white mixture over loaves.

Convection Bake in a preheated **375°F** oven about 20 minutes or until loaves sound hollow when tapped, brushing again with egg white mixture after 10 minutes. (Or, standard bake in a preheated 375°F oven for 20 to 25 minutes, brushing again with egg white mixture and rearranging baking sheets after 10 minutes.) Remove loaves from baking sheets. Cool on wire racks.
Makes 4 loaves.

■ Kneading with a Mixer ■

The yeast bread recipes in this book take advantage of the electric mixer to mix dough quickly and easily. If your stand mixer has a dough hook, you can also knead the dough in the mixer. Check the manufacturer's use and care guide to see how large a recipe your mixer can handle easily. Follow their suggestions for kneading speeds and length of time to knead.

Caramel-Pecan Rolls

Caramel-Pecan Rolls

Indulge yourself with one of these marvelous wonders. Toasting the pecans gives them a fuller, richer flavor (see tip, page 69).

4	to 4½ cups all-purpose flour, divided
1	package active dry yeast
1	cup milk
⅓	cup granulated sugar
⅓	cup butter or margarine
½	teaspoon salt
2	eggs
1¼	cups sifted powdered sugar
½	cup whipping cream
1	cup coarsely chopped pecans
3	tablespoons butter or margarine, melted
½	cup packed brown sugar
1	tablespoon ground cinnamon
¾	cup raisins (optional)

In a large mixing bowl combine *2 cups* of the flour and the yeast. In a medium saucepan heat and stir milk, granulated sugar, the ⅓ cup butter, and the salt until warm (120°F to 130°F) and butter is almost melted. Add to flour mixture; add eggs. Beat with an electric mixer on low speed for 30 seconds, scraping sides of bowl constantly. Beat on high speed for 3 minutes. Using a spoon, stir in as much of the remaining flour as you can.

Turn out onto a lightly floured surface. Knead in enough of the remaining flour to make a moderately soft dough that is smooth and elastic (3 to 5 minutes total). Shape into a ball. Place in a lightly greased bowl; turn once to grease surface. Cover and let rise in a warm place until double (about 1 hour).

Punch dough down. Turn out onto a lightly floured surface. Divide in half. Cover and let rest for 10 minutes.

For topping, in a small bowl stir together powdered sugar and whipping cream. Divide evenly between two 9x1½-inch round baking pans. Sprinkle evenly with pecans. Set pans aside.

Roll each half of the dough into a 12x8-inch rectangle. Brush each rectangle with *half* of the 3 tablespoons melted butter. Combine brown sugar and cinnamon; sprinkle *half* over each rectangle. If desired, sprinkle *half* of the raisins over each rectangle. Starting from a long side, roll up dough jelly-roll style. Seal seam. Slice each roll of dough into 12 pieces.

Place rolls, cut sides down, in pans. Cover and let rise in a warm place until nearly double (about 30 minutes).

Convection Bake in a preheated **350°F** oven for 15 to 18 minutes or until golden brown. (Or, standard bake in a preheated 375°F oven for 20 to 25 minutes.) Cool in pans on wire racks for 5 minutes. Invert onto serving plates.* Serve warm.
Makes 24 rolls.

Jumbo Caramel-Pecan Rolls: Prepare as above, *except* use a 12-inch, deep-dish pizza pan or a 13x9x2-inch baking pan. Starting from a *short side*, roll up dough jelly-roll style. Slice each into 4 pieces. Let rise as directed. **Convection Bake** in a preheated **350°F** oven for 18 to 20 minutes. (Or, standard bake in a preheated 375°F oven for 25 to 30 minutes.)
Makes 8 jumbo rolls.

*Note: If desired, wrap a pan of baked and cooled rolls in foil and freeze. To reheat, leave frozen rolls wrapped. **Convection Bake** in a preheated **350°F** oven about 35 minutes or until heated through. (Or, standard bake in a preheated 350°F oven for 35 to 40 minutes.)

Peach-Cinnamon Kuchen

This traditional German coffee cake is a delightful combination of cake and warm fruit.

- 3 cups all-purpose flour, divided
- 1 package active dry yeast
- ¾ cup milk
- ⅓ cup butter or margarine
- 1⅓ cups granulated sugar, divided
- ½ teaspoon salt
- 3 eggs
- 3 tablespoons light cream, half and half, or milk
- 1½ teaspoons ground cinnamon
- 2 cups thinly sliced peeled peaches or plums

In a large mixing bowl combine *1½ cups* of the flour and the yeast. In a saucepan heat and stir milk, butter, *⅓ cup* of the sugar, and salt until warm (120°F to 130°F) and butter is almost melted. Add to flour mixture; add *2* of the eggs. Beat with an electric mixer on low speed for 30 seconds, scraping bowl constantly. Beat on high speed 3 minutes. Using a spoon, stir in remaining flour. Dough will be very sticky.

Divide dough in half. Using a narrow spatula, spread evenly into 2 greased 9x1½-inch round and/or 9x9x2-inch baking pans, pressing dough slightly up the sides to form a rim. Cover and let rise in a warm place until double (35 to 45 minutes).

In a small bowl combine the remaining egg and the cream. Stir in the remaining 1 cup sugar and the cinnamon. Arrange the fruit on top of dough. Carefully spoon the egg mixture over fruit.

Convection Bake in a preheated **350°F** oven about 15 minutes or until golden brown. (Or, standard bake in a preheated 375°F oven for 18 to 20 minutes.)

Cool slightly. Cut into wedges or squares. Serve warm.
Makes 2 coffee cakes.

Cranberry-Pumpkin Bread

Present a loaf of this festive quick bread to a friend or neighbor for a tasty holiday gift.

- 4 cups all-purpose flour
- 2 tablespoons baking powder
- 2 teaspoons ground cinnamon
- ½ teaspoon baking soda
- ½ teaspoon ground nutmeg
- ¼ teaspoon ground ginger
- 2 cups granulated sugar
- 1 16-ounce can pumpkin
- 4 eggs
- ½ cup cooking oil
- 2 cups coarsely chopped cranberries
- ½ cup chopped almonds, toasted (see tip, page 69)
- ½ cup sifted powdered sugar
- ½ teaspoon vanilla
- 1 to 2 teaspoons milk

In a large bowl stir together flour, baking powder, cinnamon, baking soda, nutmeg, and ginger. Make a well in the center. In a medium bowl combine granulated sugar, pumpkin, eggs, and oil. Add egg mixture all at once to dry ingredients. Stir just until moistened. Fold in cranberries and almonds.

Grease bottoms and ½ inch up the sides of two 8x4x2-inch loaf pans or 9x5x3-inch loaf pans. Pour batter into pans; spread evenly.

Convection Bake in a preheated **325°F** oven for 50 to 60 minutes or until a toothpick inserted near the centers comes out clean. (Or, standard bake in a preheated 350°F oven for 60 to 65 minutes.) Cool in pans on a wire rack for 10 minutes. Remove from pans. Cool completely on wire rack. Wrap and store overnight.

For icing, mix powdered sugar and vanilla. Stir in enough of the milk to make an icing of drizzling consistency. Before serving, drizzle icing over bread.
Makes 2 loaves.

Lemon Nut Bread

This moist nut bread is great for a midmorning snack or with a salad for lunch.

- ½ cup butter or margarine
- 1 cup granulated sugar
- 2 eggs
- 1⅔ cups all-purpose flour
- ¾ cup buttermilk or sour milk (see tip, page 71)
- 1½ teaspoons finely shredded lemon peel
- ½ teaspoon baking soda
- ¼ teaspoon salt
- ⅓ cup chopped almonds, walnuts, or pecans, toasted (see tip, page 69)
- 3 tablespoons lemon juice
- 1 tablespoon granulated sugar

In a large mixing bowl beat butter with an electric mixer on medium speed about 30 seconds or until softened. Add the 1 cup sugar. Beat about 5 minutes or until light and fluffy.

Add eggs, 1 at a time, beating until combined. Add flour, buttermilk, lemon peel, baking soda, and salt. Beat just until moistened. Stir in nuts.

Grease the bottoms and ½ inch up the sides of an 8x4x2-inch loaf pan. Pour batter into pan; spread evenly.

Convection Bake in a preheated **325°F** oven for 50 to 55 minutes or until a toothpick inserted near the center comes out clean. (Or, standard bake in a preheated 350°F oven for 45 to 50 minutes. If necessary, cover loosely with foil the last 10 to 15 minutes to prevent overbrowning.) Cool in pan on a wire rack for 10 minutes. Remove from pan. Place bread on wire rack over waxed paper.

For glaze, combine lemon juice and the 1 tablespoon sugar; stir until sugar is dissolved. Spoon glaze over bread. Cool completely on wire rack.
Makes 1 loaf.

Crunchy Parmesan Corn Bread

Serve these golden morsels with chili or soup.

- 1 cup boiling water
- ¼ cup bulgur wheat
- 1 cup all-purpose flour
- 1 cup yellow cornmeal
- ⅓ cup grated Parmesan cheese
- 2 tablespoons granulated sugar
- 1 tablespoon baking powder
- ½ teaspoon dried basil, crushed
- ¼ teaspoon salt
- 2 eggs, beaten
- 1 cup milk
- ¼ cup cooking oil
- ⅓ cup drained oil-packed dried tomatoes, chopped, or drained diced pimiento
- 3 green onions, sliced (about ⅓ cup)
  Yellow cornmeal

In a small bowl pour boiling water over bulgur. Let stand for 5 minutes. Drain well; set aside. In a large bowl stir together flour, the 1 cup cornmeal, the Parmesan cheese, sugar, baking powder, basil, and salt. Make a well in the center.

In a medium bowl combine eggs, milk, and oil. Stir in bulgur. Add egg mixture all at once to dry ingredients. Stir just until moistened. Fold in tomatoes and onions.

Grease bottom and ½ inch up sides of an 8x4x2-inch or a 9x5x3-inch loaf pan. Sprinkle pan with additional cornmeal. Pour batter into pan; spread evenly.

Convection Bake in a preheated **350°F** oven for 43 to 48 minutes or until a toothpick inserted near the center comes out clean. (Or, standard bake in a preheated 375°F oven for 50 to 55 minutes. If necessary, cover loosely with foil the last 10 to 15 minutes to prevent overbrowning.)

Cool bread in pan on a wire rack for 10 minutes. Remove from pan. Serve warm.
Makes 1 loaf.

Fruit and Honey-Bran Refrigerator Muffins

Keep this batter on hand in the refrigerator so you can have fresh-baked muffins ready in a jiffy.

1½	cups all-purpose flour
1	cup whole bran cereal
¼	cup packed brown sugar
1	tablespoon baking powder
1	teaspoon ground cinnamon
¼	teaspoon salt
1	egg, beaten
1¼	cups milk
¼	cup honey
¼	cup cooking oil
½	cup raisins or chopped dried fruit (such as apricots, dates, figs, cherries, blueberries, or cranberries)

In a large bowl stir together flour, cereal, brown sugar, baking powder, cinnamon, and salt. Make a well in the center.

In a medium bowl combine egg, milk, honey, and oil. Add egg mixture all at once to dry ingredients. Stir just until moistened. Batter should be lumpy. Fold in raisins. Store in a covered container in the refrigerator for at least 2 hours or for up to 3 days.

To bake muffins, gently stir batter. Spoon batter into the desired number of greased 2½-inch muffin cups, filling each about ⅔ full.

Convection Bake in a preheated **350°F** oven for 15 to 18 minutes or until golden brown. (Or, standard bake in a preheated 400°F oven for 18 to 20 minutes.) Remove from pans. Serve warm.
Makes 12 to 14 muffins.

Cranberry-Oat Mini Muffins

Easy to eat in just a bite or two, these muffin morsels will be popular treats at the office or in your child's classroom.

¾	cup all-purpose flour
¼	cup oat bran
4	tablespoons granulated sugar, divided
1	teaspoon baking powder
	Dash salt
1	egg, beaten
⅓	cup milk
2	tablespoons cooking oil
⅓	cup chopped dried cranberries, chopped raisins, or dried currants
⅛	teaspoon ground cinnamon

In a medium bowl stir together flour, oat bran, *3 tablespoons* of the sugar, the baking powder, and salt. Make a well in the center.

In a small bowl combine egg, milk, and oil. Add egg mixture all at once to dry ingredients. Stir just until moistened. Batter should be lumpy. Fold in the cranberries.

Spoon the batter into 18 greased 1¾-inch muffin cups, filling each about ¾ full.

In a small bowl stir together the remaining 1 tablespoon sugar and the cinnamon. Sprinkle over muffins.

Convection Bake in a preheated **375°F** oven for 8 to 10 minutes or until golden brown. (Or, standard bake in a preheated 400°F oven for 12 to 15 minutes.)

Remove muffins from pans. Serve warm.
Makes 18 mini muffins.

Cranberry-Oat Mini Muffins

Applesauce-Rhubarb Muffins

  1   cup all-purpose flour
  ½   cup whole wheat flour
  1   teaspoon baking powder
1½   teaspoons ground cinnamon, divided
  ¼   teaspoon baking soda
  ¼   teaspoon salt
  1   egg, beaten
  ⅔   cup packed brown sugar
  ⅔   cup applesauce
  ¼   cup cooking oil
  ¾   cup fresh or frozen chopped rhubarb
  1   tablespoon granulated sugar

In a large bowl combine all-purpose flour, whole wheat flour, baking powder, *1 teaspoon* of the cinnamon, the baking soda, and salt. Make a well in the center.

Combine egg, brown sugar, applesauce, and oil. Add all at once to dry ingredients. Stir just until moistened. Batter should be lumpy. Fold in rhubarb.

Spoon batter into 12 greased 2½-inch muffin cups, filling each about ⅔ full. Combine granulated sugar and the remaining ½ teaspoon cinnamon. Sprinkle over muffins.

Convection Bake in a preheated **375°F** oven for 12 to 15 minutes or until golden brown. (Or, standard bake in a preheated 400°F oven for 18 to 20 minutes.) Remove from pans. Serve warm.
Makes 12 regular muffins.

Giant muffins: Prepare as above, *except* spoon batter into 6 greased 3½-inch muffin cups, filling each about ½ full. Combine granulated sugar and the remaining ½ teaspoon cinnamon. Sprinkle over muffins.
Convection Bake in a preheated **350°F** oven for 20 to 22 minutes or until firm and golden brown. (Or, standard bake in a preheated 350°F oven for 30 to 35 minutes.) Remove from pans. Serve warm.
Makes 6 large muffins.

Lemon-Poppy Seed Popovers

Add a refreshing flavor to a chicken dinner or main-dish salad with these crisp popovers hot from the oven.

  1   tablespoon shortening
  2   eggs
  1   cup milk
  1   tablespoon cooking oil
  ¾   cup all-purpose flour
  ¼   teaspoon salt
  2   teaspoons poppy seeds
1½   teaspoons finely shredded lemon peel or orange peel

Using *½ teaspoon* shortening for *each* cup, grease the bottom and sides of 6 cups of a popover pan or six 6-ounce custard cups. Place the custard cups on a baking sheet.

In a medium mixing bowl use a wire whisk or rotary beater to lightly beat eggs just until mixed. Beat in milk and oil. Add flour and salt. Beat until mixture is blended but still slightly lumpy. Stir in poppy seeds and lemon peel. Fill the greased popover or custard cups about ½ full.

Convection Bake in a preheated **375°F** oven for 30 to 35 minutes or until crusts are very firm. (Or, standard bake in a preheated 400°F oven about 40 minutes.)

Immediately after removing popovers from oven, use a fork to prick each popover to let steam escape. Turn off oven.

For crisper popovers, return popovers to the oven for 5 to 10 minutes more or until of desired crispness. (Be sure the oven is turned off.) Serve hot.
Makes 6 popovers.

Pecan-Sour Cream Coffee Ring

This tangy cake with a crunchy pecan filling is a great for a weekend breakfast or a snack.

1	cup finely chopped pecans, toasted (see tip, at right)
1/3	cup packed brown sugar
1	teaspoon ground cinnamon
2 1/2	cups all-purpose flour
1	cup granulated sugar
1	tablespoon baking powder
1/2	teaspoon salt
1/2	cup butter or margarine
3	eggs, beaten
1	8-ounce carton dairy sour cream
1/3	cup milk
1 1/4	teaspoons vanilla, divided
1	cup sifted powdered sugar
3	to 4 teaspoons milk
1/4	teaspoon rum flavoring (optional)

Generously grease a 10-inch fluted tube pan. Sprinkle *½ cup* of the pecans evenly over the bottom. For pecan filling, in a small bowl combine the remaining ½ cup pecans, the brown sugar, and cinnamon. Set pan and filling aside.

In a large bowl stir together flour, granulated sugar, baking powder, and salt. Using a pastry blender, cut in butter until the mixture resembles coarse crumbs. Make a well in the center.

In a medium bowl combine eggs, sour cream, the ⅓ cup milk, and *1 teaspoon* of the vanilla. Add egg mixture all at once to dry ingredients. Stir just until moistened. Remove *1 cup* of the batter and stir it into the pecan filling.

Spread about *1½ cups* of the plain batter into the prepared pan. Spoon the filling over batter. Carefully spoon the remaining plain batter over filling.

Convection Bake in a preheated **300°F** oven for 40 to 45 minutes or until a toothpick inserted near the center comes out clean. (Or, standard bake in a preheated 325°F oven for 45 to 50 minutes.) Cool in pan on a wire rack for 10 minutes. Invert onto a serving plate. Remove pan and cool for 15 minutes more.

For icing, in a small bowl stir together powdered sugar and the remaining ¼ teaspoon vanilla. Stir in 3 to 4 teaspoons milk to make an icing of drizzling consistency. If desired, stir in rum flavoring.

Drizzle icing over coffee cake. Serve warm. ***Makes 12 to 16 servings.***

Toasting Nuts

Keep a supply of flavorful toasted nuts on hand to use in everything from cookies and cakes to salads and main dishes. The toasted nuts will store easily in your freezer for up to a year.

To toast the nuts, spread them in a thin layer in a shallow baking pan. **Convection Bake** in a preheated **325°F** or **350°F** oven for 5 to 10 minutes or until golden brown. The convection oven bakes so evenly there's no need to stir the nuts. (Or, standard bake in a preheated 350°F oven for 5 to 10 minutes, stirring once or twice.) Cool the nuts before using or storing them.

Strawberry Ripple Tea Cake

Strawberry Ripple Tea Cake

Buttermilk gives this coffee cake a wonderful tang that blends beautifully with the strawberries.

1	10-ounce package frozen, sweetened, sliced strawberries, thawed
1	tablespoon cornstarch
2¼	cups all-purpose flour
¾	cup granulated sugar
¾	cup butter or margarine
½	teaspoon baking powder
½	teaspoon baking soda
⅛	teaspoon salt
1	egg, beaten
¾	cup buttermilk or sour milk (see tip, at right)

For filling, in a small saucepan stir together *undrained* strawberries and cornstarch until well mixed. Cook and stir over medium heat until thickened and bubbly. Remove from heat. Set aside to cool slightly.

In a large bowl stir together flour and sugar. Using a pastry blender, cut in butter until the mixture resembles coarse crumbs. Set aside *½ cup* of the flour mixture for crumb topping.

Stir baking powder, baking soda, and salt into the remaining flour mixture. Make a well in the center.

In a small bowl combine egg and buttermilk. Add egg mixture all at once to dry ingredients. Stir just until moistened.

Grease and flour a 10x2-inch round tart pan with a removable bottom or an 8x8x2-inch baking pan. Spread *two-thirds* of the batter over the bottom and about 1 inch up the sides of the prepared pan.

Carefully spread the filling over batter in pan. Spoon the remaining batter in small mounds on top of filling. Sprinkle with the crumb topping.

Convection Bake in a preheated **325°F** oven about 35 minutes or until a toothpick inserted near the center comes out clean. (Or, standard bake in a preheated 350°F oven about 35 minutes.) Cool in pan on a wire rack for 15 minutes.

Remove coffee cake from tart pan (leave in baking pan). Serve warm.
Makes 8 to 10 servings.

Making Sour Milk

If you don't have buttermilk on hand, substitute sour milk. Place 1 tablespoon of lemon juice or vinegar in a 1-cup glass measure and add enough milk to make 1 cup. Let the mixture stand for 5 minutes. Then, use the amount called for in the recipe.

Parmesan Corn Bread Puffs

A cross between muffins and corn bread, these bite-size puffs are great with soups or salads.

½	cup all-purpose flour
⅓	cup yellow cornmeal
4	teaspoons granulated sugar
1	teaspoon baking powder
⅛	teaspoon salt
1	egg, beaten
¼	cup milk
2	tablespoons cooking oil
2	tablespoons grated Parmesan cheese

In a medium bowl stir together flour, cornmeal, sugar, baking powder, and salt. Make a well in the center.

In a small bowl combine egg, milk, and oil. Add egg mixture all at once to dry ingredients. Stir just until smooth. Spoon batter into 12 greased 1¾-inch muffin cups, filling each about ¾ full.

Convection Bake in a preheated **375°F** oven for 10 to 12 minutes or until golden brown. (Or, standard bake in a preheated 400°F oven for 10 to 12 minutes.) Remove from pan. Cool on a wire rack for 5 minutes.

Place Parmesan cheese in a plastic bag. Add the warm puffs, a few at a time. Toss to coat with Parmesan cheese. Serve warm.
Makes 12 puffs.

Gruyère-Pecan Biscuits

Wow your friends or family with this elegant variation of flaky biscuits. (Pictured on the cover.)

2	cups all-purpose flour
1	tablespoon baking powder
½	teaspoon cream of tartar
½	cup butter or margarine
½	cup shredded Gruyère or Swiss cheese (2 ounces)
½	cup finely chopped pecans
⅔	cup milk

In a medium bowl stir together flour, baking powder, and cream of tartar. Using a pastry blender, cut in butter until the mixture resembles coarse crumbs.

Stir in cheese and pecans. Make a well in the center. Add milk all at once to dry ingredients. Stir just until dough clings together. Turn dough out onto a lightly floured surface.

Quickly knead dough by gently folding and pressing dough for 10 to 12 strokes or until the dough is nearly smooth. Lightly roll or pat dough to ½-inch thickness. Cut with a floured 2½-inch biscuit cutter, dipping the cutter into flour between cuts. Place biscuits on a baking sheet.

Convection Bake in a preheated **425°F** oven for 8 to 9 minutes or until golden brown. (Or, standard bake in a preheated 450°F oven for 10 to 12 minutes.) Serve hot.
Makes 10 to 12 biscuits.

Apricot Breakfast Biscuits

Have your hot bread for breakfast and sleep late, too. Just bake the biscuits ahead and wrap them in foil, seal in a plastic bag, and store at room temperature for up to 3 days. To reheat, remove the foil-wrapped biscuits from the plastic bag and **Convection Bake** *(or standard bake) in a preheated* **300°F** *oven for 10 to 12 minutes.*

2	cups all-purpose flour
1	tablespoon baking powder
¼	teaspoon salt
⅓	cup shortening
½	cup milk
⅓	cup apricot preserves or pineapple preserves
	Milk
2	teaspoons granulated sugar
⅛	teaspoon ground cinnamon

In a medium bowl stir together flour, baking powder, and salt. Using a pastry blender, cut in shortening until the mixture resembles coarse crumbs. Make a well in the center.

In a bowl combine the ½ cup milk and preserves. Add all at once to dry ingredients. Stir just until dough clings together.

Turn the dough out onto a lightly floured surface. Quickly knead dough by gently folding and pressing dough for 10 to 12 strokes or until the dough is nearly smooth. Lightly roll or pat dough to ½-inch thickness. Cut with a floured 2½-inch biscuit cutter, dipping the cutter into flour between cuts. Place biscuits on a baking sheet.

Brush tops with a little milk. In a small bowl stir together sugar and cinnamon. Sprinkle over biscuits.

Convection Bake in a preheated **425°F** oven for 7 to 10 minutes or until golden brown. (Or, standard bake in a preheated 450°F oven for 7 to 10 minutes.) Serve hot.
Makes 10 biscuits.

Savory Rosemary Scones

These incredible scones have a biscuitlike texture and go well with baked chicken, pork, or fish. (Pictured on the cover.)

2	cups all-purpose flour
1	tablespoon granulated sugar
1	tablespoon snipped fresh rosemary or 1 teaspoon dried rosemary, crushed
2	teaspoons baking powder
½	teaspoon baking soda
¼	teaspoon salt
⅛	teaspoon pepper
¼	cup butter or margarine
1	egg
1	cup dairy sour cream

In a large bowl stir together flour, sugar, rosemary, baking powder, baking soda, salt, and pepper. Using a pastry blender, cut in butter until the mixture resembles coarse crumbs. Make a well in the center.

Separate egg, reserving the egg white. In a small bowl combine egg yolk and sour cream. Add all at once to dry ingredients. Stir just until dough clings together.

Turn out onto a lightly floured surface. Quickly knead dough by gently folding and pressing dough for 10 to 12 strokes or until nearly smooth. Lightly roll or pat dough into a 7-inch circle. Cut into 12 wedges, dipping the knife into flour between cuts. Arrange wedges about 1 inch apart on a baking sheet. Brush with egg white.

Convection Bake in a preheated **375°F** oven for 9 to 11 minutes or until lightly browned. (Or, standard bake in a preheated 400°F oven for 10 to 12 minutes.) Remove from baking sheet. Cool on a wire rack for 10 minutes. Serve warm.
Makes 12 scones.

Cranberry Strudel (see recipe, page 76)

Decadent Desserts

Transform any meal into an occasion to be remembered by ending with an irresistible dessert. There's a recipe in this chapter for every affair. Try Cranberry Strudel, Honey-Almond Pie, Chocadamia Cookies, or any of our exceptional desserts in your KitchenAid® convection oven, and you'll discover new family favorites.

Lemon Curd Pastry with Mixed Berries

Elegant, but simple, this dessert combines a purchased lemon curd with a flaky puff pastry shell and fresh fruit. For a milder lemon flavor, substitute lemon pudding for the lemon curd. (Pictured on the cover.)

- 1 sheet frozen puff pastry (½ of a 17¼-ounce package), thawed
- 1 egg white, slightly beaten
- 1 teaspoon water
  Coarse sugar or granulated sugar
- ⅔ cup lemon curd (at room temperature)
- ⅔ cup dairy sour cream or plain yogurt
- ¼ teaspoon ground ginger
- 1 or 2 drops almond extract (optional)
- 3 cups fresh berries (raspberries, blueberries, and/or halved or quartered strawberries)
- 2 tablespoons honey or powdered sugar

On a lightly floured surface, unfold pastry and roll into a 15x10-inch rectangle. Cut off two ¾-inch-wide strips crosswise, then two ¾-inch-wide strips lengthwise from the rectangle. Set aside the 4 pastry strips.

Place pastry rectangle on a baking sheet. In a small bowl stir together egg white and water; brush onto rectangle. Place the 4 pastry strips on edges of rectangle to form a border and build up the sides, trimming to fit. Brush strips with egg white mixture and sprinkle with coarse sugar. Prick bottom of pastry with a fork. Cover and refrigerate for 10 to 15 minutes before baking.

Convection Roast in a preheated **375°F** oven for 14 to 16 minutes or until golden brown. (Or, standard bake in a preheated 375°F oven for 20 to 25 minutes.) Cool on a wire rack.

For filling, in a small bowl stir lemon curd until smooth. Gently stir in sour cream,

ginger, and, if desired, almond extract. Spread filling over cooled pastry. Cover and refrigerate for up to 4 hours.

Just before serving, top with desired berries. Drizzle honey or sift powdered sugar over top.
Makes 8 servings.

Cranberry Strudel

Easy-to-use frozen phyllo dough makes this impressive dessert much simpler to make than it looks. (Pictured on pages 74–75.)

- 2 cups fresh or frozen cranberries
- ¾ cup water
- ½ cup dried apples, chopped
- ½ cup chopped pecans
- ¼ cup dried currants
- ¾ cup granulated sugar
- 10 to 12 sheets frozen phyllo dough (about 9 ounces), thawed
- ⅓ cup butter or margarine, melted
- 1 egg white, slightly beaten
- 1 tablespoon water
  Powdered sugar

For filling, in a medium saucepan combine cranberries and the ¾ cup water; bring to boiling. Reduce heat and simmer, uncovered, about 5 minutes or until cranberries pop. Drain cranberries.

In a medium bowl combine drained cranberries, apples, pecans, and currants. Add granulated sugar; gently toss until mixed. Set aside.

To assemble strudel, cover a large surface with a cloth; flour cloth. Unfold phyllo dough. Stack 2 sheets of phyllo on floured cloth. (*Do not* brush butter between sheets.)

Arrange another stack of 2 sheets on the cloth, overlapping the stacks by 2 inches. Add 3 or 4 more stacks, forming a rectangle about 40x20 inches (stagger stacks so all seams are not down the middle). If necessary, trim edges evenly. Brush the phyllo dough with melted butter.

Beginning about 4 inches from a short side of dough, spoon filling in a 4-inch-wide strip across dough to within 1 inch of sides. Gently lift the 4-inch piece of dough and lay it over the filling. Slowly and evenly roll up the dough and filling, jelly-roll style, into a tight roll. If necessary, cut off excess dough from ends to within 1 inch of the filling. Fold ends under to seal.

Using 2 wide spatulas, carefully transfer strudel roll to a lightly greased 15x10x1-inch baking pan. Carefully curve the roll to form a crescent shape.

In a small bowl stir together egg white and the 1 tablespoon water. Brush mixture over top of strudel.

Convection Roast in a preheated **350°F** oven for 25 to 30 minutes or until browned. (Or, standard bake in a preheated 350°F oven for 35 to 40 minutes.)

Carefully remove strudel from pan. Cool on a wire rack. Before serving, sift powdered sugar over strudel.
Makes 12 to 16 servings.

Raspberry Truffle Cake

By mingling the flavors of chocolate and raspberry, this heavenly dessert will dazzle even the most discriminating chocolate fans.

2	8-ounce packages semisweet chocolate, cut into pieces
½	cup butter
1	tablespoon granulated sugar
1½	teaspoons all-purpose flour
1	teaspoon raspberry liqueur (optional)
4	eggs
¾	cup seedless red raspberry jam
	Whipped cream
	Fresh raspberries (optional)

In a heavy large saucepan combine chocolate and butter. Heat over low heat just until chocolate is melted, stirring constantly. Remove from heat. Stir in sugar, flour, and, if desired, raspberry liqueur. Separate eggs, reserving the egg whites. Using a wooden spoon, beat egg yolks, 1 at a time, into chocolate mixture until combined. Set aside.

In a medium mixing bowl beat egg whites with an electric mixer on high speed until stiff peaks form (tips stand straight). Fold beaten egg whites into chocolate mixture. Pour into a greased 8-inch springform pan.

Convection Bake in a preheated **325°F** oven for 18 to 22 minutes or until edges begin to puff. (Or, standard bake in a preheated 350°F oven for 25 to 30 minutes.) Cool in pan on a wire rack for 30 minutes. Remove sides of pan. Cool completely on rack. Cover and refrigerate for 4 to 24 hours.

To serve, in a small saucepan heat raspberry jam just until melted. Drizzle *1 tablespoon* jam onto each dessert plate. Top with a wedge of cake. Let stand for 20 minutes. Top with whipped cream, and, if desired, raspberries.
Makes 12 servings.

Lemon Angel Cake

Lemon Angel Cake

1½   cups egg whites (about 10 to 12 large)
1½   cups sifted powdered sugar
1   cup sifted cake flour or sifted
       all-purpose flour
1½   teaspoons cream of tartar
1   teaspoon vanilla
1   cup granulated sugar
1   teaspoon finely shredded lemon peel
       Lemon Filling (see recipe, at right)
       Powdered sugar
       Lemon slices, quartered (optional)

In a very large mixing bowl let egg whites stand at room temperature for 30 minutes.

Meanwhile, sift the 1½ cups powdered sugar and the flour together 3 times. Set aside. Add cream of tartar and vanilla to egg whites. Beat with an electric mixer on medium to high speed until soft peaks form (tips curl). Gradually add the granulated sugar, 2 tablespoons at a time, beating on medium to high speed until stiff peaks form (tips stand straight).

Sift about *one-fourth* of the flour mixture over the egg white mixture, then gently fold in. Repeat sifting and folding in the remaining flour mixture, using one-fourth of it each time. Gently fold in lemon peel. Gently pour batter evenly into an *ungreased* 10-inch tube pan. Gently cut through batter with a metal spatula.

Convection Bake in a preheated **325°F** oven about 40 minutes or until top springs back when lightly touched. (Or, standard bake in a preheated 350°F oven for 40 to 45 minutes.) Immediately invert the cake in pan. Cool completely.

Meanwhile, prepare Lemon Filling. Using a narrow metal spatula, loosen sides of cake from pan. Remove cake from pan. Using a serrated knife, cut off the top 1 inch of the cake; set aside. With knife held parallel to side of cake, cut around the hole in center, leaving a 1-inch thickness of cake around hole and cutting to within 1 inch of bottom of cake. Cut around the inside of outer edge of cake, leaving the outer cake wall 1 inch thick and cutting to within 1 inch of bottom of cake. Using a fork or spoon, remove center of cake, leaving a 1-inch-thick base.

Place cake on a serving plate. Spoon filling into hollowed-out section. Replace top of cake. Cover and refrigerate for 4 to 24 hours. Before serving, sift powdered sugar over cake. If desired, garnish with lemon slices. *Makes 12 servings.*

Lemon Filling

¾   cup granulated sugar
1   envelope unflavored gelatin (2¼ teaspoons)
       Dash salt
1   cup cold water
2   teaspoons finely shredded lemon peel
3   tablespoons lemon juice
       Few drops yellow food coloring
1   cup whipping cream

In a small saucepan stir together sugar, gelatin, and salt. Gradually stir in water. Stir in lemon peel and juice. Heat and stir just until gelatin is dissolved. If desired, stir in food coloring.

Cool gelatin mixture in a bath of ice water, stirring constantly, for 5 to 8 minutes or until mixture is the consistency of corn syrup. Remove from ice water; set aside.

In a chilled medium mixing bowl beat whipping cream until soft peaks form. Fold about *one-fourth* of the whipped cream into the gelatin mixture. Gradually pour the gelatin mixture over the remaining whipped cream, folding to combine. Refrigerate about 5 minutes or until the mixture mounds when spooned. *Makes 3 cups.*

Fall Apple Cake

1¼   cups granulated sugar
½   cup cooking oil
2   eggs
2   teaspoons vanilla
1   cup apple juice or apple cider
2   cups all-purpose flour
¾   cup whole wheat flour
2   teaspoons baking powder
2   teaspoons ground cinnamon
1   teaspoon ground nutmeg
½   teaspoon baking soda
3   cups peeled, cored, and sliced
     cooking apples
½   cup finely chopped walnuts, toasted
     (see tip, page 69)
¾   cup sifted powdered sugar
2   tablespoons frozen apple juice concentrate,
     thawed, or 1 tablespoon apple juice or
     apple cider

In a large mixing bowl beat granulated sugar and oil with an electric mixer on medium speed until combined. Add eggs and vanilla. Beat on medium speed about 1 minute or until creamy. Stir in apple juice.

Stir together all-purpose flour, whole wheat flour, baking powder, cinnamon, nutmeg, and baking soda. Stir into egg mixture. Gently stir in apples and walnuts. Pour batter into a greased and lightly floured 10-inch tube pan.

Convection Bake in a preheated **325°F** oven about 50 minutes or until a toothpick inserted near the center comes out clean. (Or, standard bake in a preheated 350°F oven for 60 to 65 minutes.) Cool in pan on a wire rack for 10 minutes. Remove cake from pan. Cool on wire rack for 15 minutes.

For glaze, combine powdered sugar and enough of the apple juice concentrate to make a glaze of thin drizzling consistency. Brush glaze over top and sides of cake. Serve warm.
Makes 12 servings.

Raspberry-Pear Pie

So simple, yet so good, this fruit pie is hard to beat when you want a satisfying dessert.

½   cup granulated sugar
¼   cup all-purpose flour
5   cups peeled, cored, and thinly sliced pears
1   cup fresh raspberries
     Pastry for Double-Crust Pie (see recipe,
     opposite page)

In a large bowl stir together sugar and flour. Add pears and gently toss until fruit is well coated with sugar mixture. Gently stir in raspberries.

Prepare Pastry for Double-Crust Pie. Transfer fruit mixture to the pastry-lined pie plate. Trim the bottom pastry to the edge of the pie plate. Cut slits in the top crust. Place the top crust on filling. Trim top crust ½ inch beyond edge of pie plate. Fold top crust under bottom pastry. Seal and crimp edge of pastry.

Convection Roast in a preheated **375°F** oven for 40 to 45 minutes or until golden brown. (Or, standard bake in a preheated 375°F oven for 50 to 60 minutes. Cover the edge of pie with foil the first 25 minutes, then remove foil and continue baking.) Serve warm.
Makes 8 servings.

Deep-Dish Apple Pie

    10 cups peeled, cored, and thinly sliced
        cooking apples
    ⅔   cup granulated sugar
    ½   cup raisins
    2   tablespoons all-purpose flour
    1¼ teaspoons apple pie spice, divided
    5   tablespoons butter or margarine, divided
        Whole Wheat Pastry (see recipe variation,
        at right)
    1   tablespoon milk
    1   tablespoon granulated sugar
    4   teaspoons cornstarch
    1½ cups apple cider or apple juice
    ⅓   cup packed brown sugar
    2   tablespoons dark rum (optional)

In a very large bowl toss together apples, the
⅔ cup granulated sugar, the raisins, flour,
and *1 teaspoon* of the apple pie spice.
Transfer to a 2-quart rectangular baking
dish. Dot with *1 tablespoon* of the butter.

Prepare Whole Wheat Pastry. On a lightly
floured surface, roll dough into a 13x9-inch
rectangle. Place on top of fruit. Trim pastry
to ½ inch beyond edges of dish. Fold under
extra pastry; crimp edges to sides of dish.
Cut slits in pastry. Brush with milk; sprinkle
with the 1 tablespoon granulated sugar.

Convection Roast in a preheated **350°F**
oven 35 to 40 minutes or until golden brown.
(Or, standard bake in a preheated 375°F
oven for 45 to 50 minutes. Cover edges with
foil the first 25 minutes; remove foil and
continue baking.)

For sauce, in a small saucepan, melt the
remaining 4 tablespoons butter. Stir in
cornstarch and the remaining ¼ teaspoon pie
spice. Add cider, brown sugar, and, if desired,
rum. Cook and stir until bubbly. Cook and
stir 2 minutes more. Serve with warm pie.
Makes 8 servings.

Pastry for Single-Crust Pie

    1¼ cups all-purpose flour
    ¼   teaspoon salt
    ⅓   cup shortening
    4   to 5 tablespoons cold water

In a medium bowl stir together flour and
salt. Using a pastry blender, cut in
shortening until the pieces are the size of
small peas.

Sprinkle cold water, *1 tablespoon* at a
time, over mixture, tossing with a fork after
each addition until all is moistened. Form
dough into a ball. On a lightly floured
surface, flatten dough with hands. Roll
dough into a 12-inch circle. Fit pastry into a
9-inch pie plate, being careful not to stretch
pastry. Trim to ½ inch beyond edge of pie
plate; fold under extra pastry. Flute edge.
Bake as directed in pie recipe.

Whole Wheat Pastry: Prepare pastry as
above, *except* use ¾ *cup* all-purpose flour
and ½ cup *whole wheat flour.*

Pastry for Double-Crust Pie

    2   cups all-purpose flour
    ½   teaspoon salt
    ⅔   cup shortening
    6   to 7 tablespoons cold water

In a large bowl stir together flour and salt.
Using a pastry blender, cut in shortening
until the pieces are the size of small peas.

Sprinkle cold water, *1 tablespoon* at a
time, over mixture, tossing with a fork after
each addition until all is moistened. Divide
dough in half. Form each half into a ball.

On a lightly floured surface, roll 1 ball of
dough into a 12-inch circle. Fit pastry into a
9-inch pie plate, being careful not to stretch
pastry. For top crust, roll out remaining
dough. Continue as directed in pie recipe.

Honey-Almond Pie

A dollop of amaretto whipped cream makes this variation of pecan pie truly magnificent.

Pastry for Single-Crust Pie (see recipe, page 81)
3   eggs
¾   cup granulated sugar
½   cup light corn syrup
⅓   cup butter or margarine, melted
¼   cup honey
3   tablespoons amaretto or ¾ teaspoon almond extract, divided
1   cup sliced almonds, toasted (see tip, page 69)
1   cup whipping cream
2   tablespoons powdered sugar
½   teaspoon vanilla

Prepare Pastry for Single-Crust Pie. On a lightly floured surface, roll dough into a 12-inch circle.

Fit pastry into a 9-inch pie plate, being careful not to stretch pastry. Trim to ½ inch beyond edge of pie plate; fold under extra pastry. Make a high fluted edge.

For filling, in a medium mixing bowl use a rotary beater or wire whisk to lightly beat eggs just until mixed. Stir in granulated sugar, corn syrup, melted butter, honey, and *1 tablespoon* of the amaretto or *¼ teaspoon* of the almond extract. Mix well. Stir in almonds.

Set the pastry shell on oven rack. Carefully pour filling into pastry shell.

Convection Roast in a preheated **325°F** oven for 40 to 45 minutes or until a knife inserted near the center comes out clean. (Or, standard bake in a preheated 350°F oven for 45 to 50 minutes. Cover edge of pie with foil the first 35 minutes, then remove foil and continue baking.) Cool on a rack.

In a chilled medium mixing bowl combine whipping cream, powdered sugar, the remaining 2 tablespoons amaretto or ½ teaspoon almond extract, and the vanilla. Beat with an electric mixer on low speed until soft peaks form (tips curl). Serve with pie. Cover pie and refrigerate to store. *Makes 8 servings.*

Mince-Peach Pie

Dress up a two-crust pie by cutting a decorative shape, such as a heart or an apple, from the pastry scraps. Then brush one side of the cutout with water and position it on the top of the pie before baking.

1   29-ounce can peach slices, drained
1   27-ounce jar (2⅔ cups) mincemeat
    Pastry for Double-Crust Pie (see recipe, page 81)
    Milk
    Vanilla ice cream (optional)

Cut peaches into large chunks. In a large bowl stir together peaches and mincemeat. Set aside.

Prepare Pastry for Double-Crust Pie. Transfer fruit mixture to the pastry-lined pie plate. Trim the bottom pastry to the edge of the pie plate. Cut slits in the top crust (if desired, use a miniature cookie cutter). Place top crust on filling. Trim top crust ½ inch beyond edge of pie plate. Fold top crust under bottom pastry. Seal and crimp edge of pastry. Brush with a little milk.

Convection Roast in a preheated **375°F** oven about 50 minutes or until golden brown. (Or, standard bake in a preheated 375°F oven about 50 minutes. Cover edge of pie with foil the first 25 minutes, then remove foil and continue baking.)

Serve warm. If desired, serve with ice cream. *Makes 8 servings.*

Mince-Peach Pie

Chocadamia Cookies

These yummy chocolate and macadamia nut drops will keep their fresh-from-the-oven goodness if you store them in a tightly covered container or a sealed plastic bag.

½	cup butter or margarine
½	cup packed brown sugar
¼	cup granulated sugar
¼	teaspoon baking soda
	Dash salt
1	egg
1	tablespoon water
1	teaspoon vanilla
1¼	cups all-purpose flour
1⅓	cups semisweet chocolate chunks
1	cup macadamia nuts or walnuts, coarsely chopped

In a large mixing bowl beat butter with an electric mixer on medium speed about 30 seconds or until softened.

Add brown sugar, granulated sugar, baking soda, and salt. Beat until thoroughly combined, scraping the sides of bowl occasionally. Beat in egg, water, and vanilla until combined.

Beat in as much of the flour as you can with the mixer. Stir in any remaining flour with a spoon. Stir in chocolate chunks and nuts. Drop dough by rounded teaspoons about 2 inches apart onto cookie sheets.

Convection Bake in a preheated **325°F** oven about 9 minutes or until tops are light golden brown and set. (Or, standard bake in a preheated 375°F oven for 9 to 10 minutes.) Cool on cookie sheets for 1 minute. Remove cookies from sheets. Cool completely on wire racks.
Makes about 36 cookies.

■ Hints for Baking with Margarine ■

If you plan to use margarine when making cookies, crisps, cobblers, and other baked goods, the type of margarine you use will make a difference in the finished product.

For the best results always use a stick product that is labeled "margarine," not "spread." It also should contain no less than 60 percent vegetable oil. Products with less vegetable oil have more water, which affects the texture and quality of baked goods. For example, cookies or toppers for crisps made with light margarine or spread will be soggy rather than crisp.

Also, cookie doughs made with corn oil margarine will be softer than those made with butter. For shaped or sliced cookie doughs made with corn oil margarine, chill the dough in the freezer instead of the refrigerator for at least 2 hours. For cutout cookie dough, refrigerate dough at least 5 hours before rolling it out.

Brown Sugar-Hazelnut Rounds

These superb slice-and-bake cookies bake up crisp on the outside and chewy on the inside in the convection oven.

- ½ cup shortening
- ½ cup butter or margarine
- 1¼ cups packed brown sugar
- ½ teaspoon baking soda
- 1 egg
- 1 teaspoon vanilla
- 2½ cups all-purpose flour
- ¾ cup ground toasted hazelnuts or pecans
- ⅔ cup finely chopped, toasted hazelnuts or pecans (optional)
- 1½ cups milk chocolate pieces (optional)
- 4 teaspoons shortening (optional)
  Finely chopped, toasted hazelnuts or pecans (optional)

In a large mixing bowl beat the ½ cup shortening and the butter with an electric mixer on medium speed about 30 seconds or until softened.

Add brown sugar and baking soda. Beat until thoroughly combined, scraping sides of bowl occasionally. Beat in egg and vanilla until combined. Beat in as much of the flour as you can with the mixer. Stir in any remaining flour and the ¾ cup ground nuts with a spoon.

On waxed paper, shape dough into two 10-inch rolls. If desired, roll logs in the ⅔ cup finely chopped nuts. Wrap each in waxed paper or plastic wrap. Refrigerate for 4 to 48 hours or until firm enough to slice.

With a thin-bladed knife, cut dough into ¼-inch-thick slices. Place slices about 1 inch apart on cookie sheets.

Convection Bake in a preheated **325°F** oven for 6 to 8 minutes or until edges are firm. (Or, standard bake in a preheated 375°F oven about 10 minutes.) Remove from sheets. Cool on wire racks.

If desired, in a heavy small saucepan combine chocolate and the 4 teaspoons shortening. Heat over low heat just until melted, stirring constantly. Remove from heat. Drizzle cookies with melted chocolate. If desired, sprinkle with additional nuts. **Makes about 60 cookies.**

Shortbread Cutout Cookies

Dipping the cookie cutter into flour before cutting out each cookie will help keep it from sticking to the cutter.

- 1¼ cups all-purpose flour
- 3 tablespoons granulated sugar
- ½ cup butter
  Milk (optional)
  Coarse sugar (optional)

In a medium bowl stir together flour and granulated sugar. Using a pastry blender, cut in butter until the mixture resembles fine crumbs and starts to cling together. Form the mixture into a ball. Knead in the bowl about 1 minute or until smooth.

On a lightly floured surface, roll dough to ¼-inch thickness. Using desired cookie cutters or a knife, cut into 2- to 2½-inch shapes, rerolling and cutting trimmings as necessary. If desired, brush cutouts with milk and sprinkle with coarse sugar. Place on cookie sheets.

Convection Bake in a preheated **325°F** oven about 10 minutes or until bottoms just start to brown. (Or, standard bake in a preheated 325°F oven for 14 to 16 minutes.) Remove from cookie sheets. Cool on racks. **Makes 18 to 24 cookies.**

Viennese Raspberry Squares

Viennese Raspberry Squares

Based on the classic Austrian dessert, Linzer Torte, these appealing squares melt in your mouth.

- 2 eggs
- ⅓ cup butter or margarine
- ⅓ cup granulated sugar
- 1 cup all-purpose flour
- ¼ teaspoon cream of tartar
- ⅔ cup sifted powdered sugar
- 1 cup finely chopped almonds or walnuts, toasted (see tip, page 69)
- ½ cup red raspberry or apricot preserves

Separate eggs, reserving egg yolks. In a medium mixing bowl let egg whites stand at room temperature for 30 minutes. Set aside.

For crust, in another medium mixing bowl beat butter with an electric mixer on medium speed about 30 seconds or until softened. Add granulated sugar and egg yolks. Beat until thoroughly combined, scraping bowl occasionally. Beat in as much flour as you can with the mixer. Stir in any remaining flour with a spoon. Mixture will be thick. Press onto the bottom of a 9x9x2-inch baking pan.

Convection Bake in a preheated **325°F** oven about 15 minutes or until light golden brown. (Or, standard bake in a preheated 350°F oven about 15 minutes.)

Meanwhile, thoroughly wash and dry beaters. For meringue topping, add cream of tartar to egg whites. Beat on medium speed until soft peaks form (tips curl). Gradually add powdered sugar, beating until stiff peaks form (tips stand straight). Gently fold in nuts. Spread preserves over hot baked crust. Carefully spread meringue topping over preserves.

Convection Bake for 15 to 20 minutes more or until topping is golden brown. (Or, standard bake for 15 to 20 minutes more.) Cool in pan on a wire rack. Cut into squares. Cover and refrigerate to store.
Makes 36 bars.

Raisin-Filled Oatmeal Bars

These tasty old-fashioned bars are always popular with kids and grownups alike.

- ½ cup water
- 2 tablespoons granulated sugar
- 2 teaspoons cornstarch
- 1 cup raisins
- 1 cup all-purpose flour
- 1 cup quick-cooking rolled oats
- ⅔ cup packed brown sugar
- ¼ teaspoon baking soda
- ½ cup butter or margarine

For filling, in a medium saucepan combine water, granulated sugar, and cornstarch. Add raisins. Cook and stir over medium heat until thickened and bubbly. Set aside.

In a medium bowl combine flour, oats, brown sugar, and baking soda. Using a pastry blender, cut in butter until the mixture resembles coarse crumbs. Reserve ½ cup of the flour mixture. Press the remaining flour mixture onto the bottom of a 9x9x2-inch baking pan. Spread with filling. Sprinkle with the reserved flour mixture.

Convection Bake in a preheated **325°F** oven for 20 to 25 minutes or until the top is golden brown. (Or, standard bake in a preheated 350°F oven for 30 to 35 minutes.)

Cool in pan on a wire rack. Cut into bars.
Makes 24 bar cookies.

Apple Bread Pudding

- 1 cup dried apples, chopped
- 4 eggs
- 2¼ cups milk
- ½ cup granulated sugar
- ½ teaspoon ground cinnamon
- ½ teaspoon vanilla
- ⅛ teaspoon ground nutmeg
- 2½ cups dry whole wheat bread cubes*
- ¼ cup butter or margarine
- ½ cup packed brown sugar
- 1 tablespoon light corn syrup
- ¼ cup whipping cream
- ¼ cup chopped pecans

In a small bowl pour enough boiling water over dried apples to cover. Let stand for 5 minutes. Drain well. In a large mixing bowl use a rotary beater or wire whisk to beat eggs, milk, granulated sugar, cinnamon, vanilla, and nutmeg until combined.

In a 2-quart square baking dish toss together bread cubes and apples. Pour the egg mixture evenly over bread mixture.

Convection Bake in a preheated **325°F** oven about 30 minutes or until a knife inserted near the center comes out clean. Some areas near the center will appear soft set. (Or, standard bake in a preheated 350°F oven for 35 to 40 minutes.)

For sauce, melt butter. Stir in brown sugar and corn syrup. Cook and stir until mixture comes to a full boil. Stir in cream. Return to a full boil. Remove from heat. Stir in pecans. Serve sauce over warm bread pudding.
Makes 6 to 8 servings.

*Note: To dry bread, spread about 3 cups *fresh bread cubes* in a shallow baking pan. **Convection Bake** in a preheated **300°F** oven for 5 to 8 minutes or until dry, stirring once. (Or, standard bake in a preheated 300°F oven 10 to 15 minutes, stirring twice.)

Rhubarb-Pineapple Crisp

Tangy fruit filling plus a crunchy nut topping equals one splendid dessert.

- 7 cups fresh or frozen rhubarb cut into 1-inch pieces
- 1 8-ounce can crushed pineapple, drained
- 1½ cups packed brown sugar, divided
- 2 tablespoons cornstarch
- 2 teaspoons finely shredded lemon peel
- ½ cup rolled oats
- ½ cup all-purpose flour
- ¼ cup butter or margarine
- ¼ cup chopped pecans
- 1 tablespoon chopped candied ginger
  Vanilla ice cream (optional)

Thaw rhubarb, if frozen, and drain well. In a large bowl combine fresh or thawed rhubarb, pineapple, and *1 cup* of the brown sugar. Let stand for 15 minutes for thawed fruit or 1 hour for fresh fruit. Drain mixture, reserving juices. If necessary, add water to reserved juices to equal ⅔ cup.

Place the ⅔ cup reserved juices in a small saucepan. Stir in cornstarch. Cook and stir over medium heat until thickened and bubbly. Remove from heat. Stir into the rhubarb mixture. Stir in lemon peel. Pour mixture into a 2-quart square baking dish.

For topping, combine oats, flour, and the remaining ½ cup brown sugar. Using a pastry blender, cut in butter until the mixture resembles coarse crumbs. Stir in pecans and ginger. Spoon over rhubarb mixture.

Convection Bake in a preheated **350°F** oven about 40 minutes or until lightly browned and bubbly. (Or, standard bake in a preheated 350°F oven about 1 hour.)

Serve warm. If desired, serve with ice cream.
Makes 6 to 8 servings.

Peach Dumplings with Brandy Sauce

Show off the capabilities of your convection oven by baking these dumplings. The pastry turns out beautifully golden brown.

1½	cups water
1	cup granulated sugar, divided
¼	teaspoon ground cinnamon
¼	teaspoon ground nutmeg
2	tablespoons butter or margarine
	Pastry for Double-Crust Pie (see recipe, page 81)
4	medium peaches, peeled, halved, and pitted
2	tablespoons raisins
2	tablespoons finely chopped nuts
1	egg, beaten
¾	cup whipping cream
1	tablespoon brandy or apple juice

For syrup, in a medium saucepan combine water, ¾ *cup* of the sugar, the cinnamon, and nutmeg. Bring to boiling. Stir in butter until melted. Remove from heat; set aside.

Prepare Pastry for Double-Crust Pie, except form the dough into 1 ball. On a lightly floured surface, roll dough into a 14-inch square. Cut the pastry into four 7-inch squares.

Place a peach half, cut side up, in the center of each pastry square. In a small bowl combine raisins and nuts. Spoon raisin mixture into the centers of peaches. Place the remaining peaches on top of the filled halves.

Moisten edges of pastry with water. Fold corners to the center on top of the peaches, pinching edges together to seal. Place dumplings in a 2-quart square baking dish. Pour the syrup over dumplings.

Convection Roast in a preheated **375°F** oven for 35 to 40 minutes or until pastry is golden brown and syrup is bubbly. (Or, standard bake in a preheated 375°F oven about 45 minutes.) Let the dumplings cool about 30 minutes before serving.

Meanwhile, for sauce, in a small saucepan combine egg, whipping cream, and the remaining ¼ cup sugar. Cook and stir over medium heat until the mixture is thickened and starting to simmer. *Do not boil.*

Remove from heat. Stir in brandy. Serve warm sauce over dumplings.

Makes 4 servings.

Cherry Cobbler

Cherry Cobbler

The secret to a perfect flaky biscuit topping is to have the fruit filling bubbling hot when you drop the dough onto the filling.

- ½ cup all-purpose flour
- 2 tablespoons granulated sugar
- ¾ teaspoon baking powder
- ⅛ teaspoon salt
- 3 tablespoons butter or margarine
- ¾ cup granulated sugar
- 2 tablespoons cornstarch
- 4 cups fresh or frozen unsweetened, pitted, tart red cherries
- ⅓ cup water
- 3 tablespoons milk
- 1 tablespoon coarse sugar (optional)

For biscuit topping, in a medium bowl stir together flour, the 2 tablespoons granulated sugar, the baking powder, and salt. Using a pastry blender, cut in butter until the mixture resembles coarse crumbs. Make a well in the center; set aside.

For filling, in a medium saucepan combine the ¾ cup granulated sugar and the cornstarch. Add cherries and water. Cook and stir over medium heat until slightly thickened and bubbly. Reduce heat and keep hot. Add milk all at once to dry ingredients. Stir just until moistened.

Transfer *hot* filling to a 1½-quart round casserole. Immediately spoon biscuit topping into 4 mounds on top of filling. If desired, sprinkle biscuit topping with coarse sugar.

Convection Bake in a preheated **375°F** oven for 18 to 20 minutes or until a toothpick inserted into biscuit topping comes out clean. (Or, standard bake in a preheated 400°F oven about 20 minutes.) Serve warm. *Makes 4 servings.*

Fresh Fruit Meringue Shells

For easy entertaining, make the crisp meringue shells several days ahead and prepare the fruit a few hours before serving.

- 3 egg whites
- 1 teaspoon vanilla
- ¼ teaspoon cream of tartar
- 1 cup granulated sugar
- 2 tablespoons apricot, pineapple, or strawberry preserves
- 1 tablespoon brandy or orange juice
- 3 cups fresh fruit (blueberries, sliced strawberries, halved grapes, and/or cut-up melon, mango, or papaya)

Cover a baking sheet with plain brown or parchment paper. Draw eight 3-inch circles on the paper. For meringue, in a large mixing bowl combine egg whites, vanilla, and cream of tartar. Beat with an electric mixer on medium speed until soft peaks form (tips curl). Add sugar, 2 tablespoons at a time, beating on high speed about 7 minutes or until very stiff peaks form (tips stand straight) and sugar is almost dissolved.

Pipe the meringue through a pastry tube onto the circles on the paper, building up the sides to form shells. Or, use the back of a spoon to spread the meringue over circles, building up the sides.

Convection Bake in a preheated **300°F** oven for 35 minutes. (Or, standard bake in a preheated 300°F oven for 35 minutes.) Turn off oven. Let shells dry in the oven, with door closed, for at least 1 hour. (Be sure the oven is turned off.) Remove shells. Store in an airtight container for up to 1 week.

To serve, combine preserves and brandy. Toss with fruit. Spoon into meringue shells. *Makes 8 servings.*

Lemon Gingerbread Soufflé

A favorite flavor combination—lemon with spicy gingerbread—goes light and airy in this first-class dessert.

	Butter or margarine
	Granulated sugar
3	tablespoons butter or margarine
3	tablespoons all-purpose flour
¾	cup milk
4	eggs
1	teaspoon finely shredded lemon peel
1	tablespoon lemon juice
½	cup packed brown sugar, divided
1	teaspoon ground ginger
½	teaspoon ground cinnamon
¼	teaspoon ground nutmeg
⅛	teaspoon ground cloves
¼	teaspoon cream of tartar
	Whipped cream (optional)

Butter the sides of a 2-quart soufflé dish. Coat the sides with granulated sugar. Set dish aside.

In a small saucepan melt the 3 tablespoons butter. Stir in flour. Add milk all at once. Cook and stir over medium heat until thickened and bubbly. Mixture will be very thick.

Separate eggs, reserving the egg whites. In a medium bowl beat egg yolks. Gradually stir thickened milk mixture into yolks. Stir in lemon peel and lemon juice. Gradually add ¼ *cup* of the brown sugar, the ginger, cinnamon, nutmeg, and cloves, stirring until smooth. Set aside.

In a large mixing bowl combine egg whites and cream of tartar. Beat with an electric mixer on medium speed until soft peaks form (tips curl). Gradually add the remaining ¼ cup brown sugar, beating until stiff peaks form (tips stand straight).

Gently fold about ½ *cup* of the beaten egg whites into the egg yolk mixture. Gradually pour the yolk mixture over the remaining egg whites, folding to combine. Pour into the prepared soufflé dish.

Convection Bake in a preheated **325°F** oven about 40 minutes or until a knife inserted near the center comes out clean. (Or, standard bake in a preheated 350°F oven for 40 to 45 minutes.)

Serve soufflé immediately. If desired, top with whipped cream.
Makes 6 servings.

Brandied Cream Puffs

These cream puffs are also marvelous filled with chicken or shrimp salad for lunch.

- 1 cup water
- ½ cup butter or margarine
- ⅛ teaspoon salt
- 1 cup all-purpose flour
- 6 eggs
- ¾ cup granulated sugar
- 3 tablespoons cornstarch or ⅓ cup all-purpose flour
- 3 cups milk
- 1 tablespoon butter or margarine
- 1 to 2 tablespoons brandy or 1½ teaspoons vanilla
  Powdered sugar

In a medium saucepan combine water, the ½ cup butter, and the salt. Bring to boiling.

Add the 1 cup flour all at once, stirring vigorously. Cook and stir until the mixture forms a ball that does not separate. Remove from heat. Cool for 5 minutes. Add *4* of the eggs, 1 at a time, beating with a spoon after each addition until smooth. Drop 10 heaping tablespoons of batter about 3 inches apart onto a greased baking sheet.

Convection Bake in a preheated **375°F** oven about 30 minutes or until golden brown. (Or, standard bake in a preheated 400°F oven about 30 minutes.) Remove from oven. Split puffs and remove any soft dough from the insides. Cool on a wire rack.

Meanwhile, for filling, in a heavy medium saucepan combine granulated sugar and cornstarch. Add milk all at once. Cook and stir over medium heat until mixture is thickened and bubbly. Cook and stir for 2 minutes more. Remove from heat.

In a medium bowl beat the remaining 2 eggs. Gradually stir about *1 cup* of the hot mixture into beaten eggs. Return all of the egg mixture to the saucepan.

Cook until nearly bubbly, but *do not boil.* Reduce heat. Cook and stir for 2 minutes more. Remove from heat.

Stir in the 1 tablespoon butter and the brandy. Pour filling into a bowl. Cover the surface with clear plastic wrap and refrigerate. *Do not stir.*

To serve, spoon chilled filling into cream puffs. Replace the tops of cream puffs. Sift powdered sugar over tops.
Makes 10 servings.

Index